Cooking for a
Healthy Heart

Jacqui Lynas

hamlyn

The Family Heart Association (FHA) is an organization for families who have Familial Hypercholesterolaemia (FH) and other inherited forms of hyperlipidaemia. FH is the most common disorder, affecting 1 in 500 of the population. It is an inherited genetic disorder of cholesterol metabolism, resulting in high cholesterol levels and the likelihood of early death from heart disease. The FHA aims to provide support and encouragement for FH families. If affected families can be identified, screened, diagnosed and treated, then unnecessary tragedies can be prevented and lives saved. You can make a positive difference to your own well-being and to the future of The Family Heart Association. Please help by joining the FHA. At just £1 a month it is excellent value. You will receive the Family Heart Digest magazine every two months and have access to the members section of the website. The magazine keeps healthcare professionals and the public right up-to-date with heart disease, with a particular focus on cholesterol.

Family Heart Association, 7 North Road, Maidenhead, Berkshire SL6 1PE
Tel: 01628 628638
Website: www.familyheart.org
Email: fha@familyheart.org

This book is for my Dad who is a 'great cooker!'

First published in Great Britain in 2002 by
Hamlyn, a division of Octopus Publishing Group Ltd
2–4 Heron Quays, London E14 4JP

Copyright © Octopus Publishing Group Ltd 2004

This revised edition published in 2004

ISBN 0 600 61051 9

A CIP catalogue record for this book is available from the British Library

Printed and bound in China

10 9 8 7 6 5 4 3 2

The publisher has taken all reasonable care in the preparation of this book but the information it contains is not intended to take the place of treatment by a qualified medical practitioner.

NOTES
Both metric and imperial measurements are given for the recipes. Use one set of measures only, not a mixture of both.
    A few recipes include nuts and nut derivatives. Anyone with a known nut allergy must avoid these.
    Free-range medium eggs should be used unless otherwise stated. The Department of Health advises that eggs should not be consumed raw. It is prudent for more vulnerable people, such as pregnant and nursing mothers, invalids, the elderly, babies and young children, to avoid uncooked or lightly cooked dishes made with eggs.
    Meat and poultry should be cooked thoroughly. To test if poultry is cooked, pierce the flesh through the thickest part with a skewer or fork - the juices should run clear, never pink or red.
    All the recipes in this book have been analyzed by the author. The analysis refers to each serving, unless otherwise stated.

Contents

Introduction

Heart disease is now established as the number one killer in the world, claiming more than six million people each year. Nearly all deaths from heart disease are as a result of a heart attack or 'myocardial infarction'. About half of all heart attacks are fatal, and in about a third of them death occurs before reaching hospital. In the UK, heart disease will claim a victim every three minutes, and in the USA, every single minute. Many deaths are premature and family, friends and colleagues are all affected by the tragedy. For those who are lucky enough to survive a heart attack, life is never quite the same again. Heart disease has developed into a lethal epidemic and the problem is set to continue as people live longer and have unhealthy lifestyles.

Yet heart disease is potentially avoidable and preventable. If you want to beat heart disease, rethinking your lifestyle can help reduce many of the risk factors of heart disease such as high cholesterol, high blood pressure, diabetes, smoking and being overweight. If you already have heart disease, it is never too late to re-evaluate your lifestyle, and there is overwhelming evidence that changing your eating habits can save your life.

Dietary advice can be all too confusing, given that we are being bombarded by often conflicting messages, but that is because the effect of diet is complex and there is still much to discover. Simply advocating a low-fat diet is no longer adequate, and current interest is focused on the benefits of a broad-based, multi-faceted dietary approach. This book clearly and concisely explains the latest dietary advice from medical and nutritional experts to help you eat for a healthy heart, and its recommendations are based on consensus opinion and sound scientific research.

How Your Heart Works

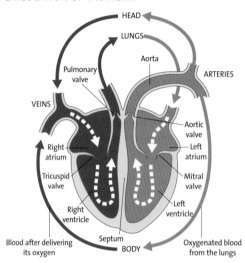

HEAD

LUNGS

Aorta

Pulmonary valve

ARTERIES

VEINS

Aortic valve

Right atrium

Left atrium

Tricuspid valve

Mitral valve

Right ventricle

Left ventricle

Blood after delivering its oxygen

Septum

BODY

Oxygenated blood from the lungs

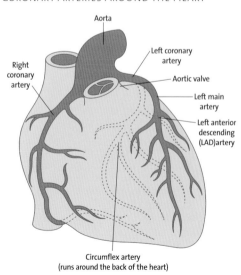

Aorta

Left coronary artery

Right coronary artery

Aortic valve

Left main artery

Left anterior descending (LAD)artery

Circumflex artery
(runs around the back of the heart)

A Strong Heart for a Long Life

The heart is the powerhouse of the body, driving blood to all the organs in your body. It is a massively strong muscle and is about the size of a clenched fist. It beats tirelessly, 60 to 80 times a minute (and more if you do anything energetic), day and night, pumping out between five and 20 litres ($8^3/_4$ and 35 pints) of blood every minute, depending on your body's needs.

We feel each heartbeat or contraction of the heart muscle as the pulse. The medical term for this contraction is systole. Diastole describes the relaxation of the heart between beats. The heart has two pairs of chambers, two on the right and two on the left. The right half of the heart pumps blood through the lungs to pick up oxygen, and the left half of the heart pumps oxygen-rich blood, returning from the lungs, to the rest of the body.

Coronary Arteries

To do all this work, the heart muscle itself needs fuel and oxygen for energy, and it gets this from its own blood supply. The blood vessels that supply the heart are called coronary arteries. They need to be tough to cope with the pressure of the beating heart.

Physical Fitness

The size of the heart and how efficiently it beats depend upon your physical fitness. People who exercise regularly have larger, stronger hearts that beat more slowly to deliver the same amount of blood as the heart of a less fit person. You can lower your pulse rate by increasing your exercise levels – ideally, brisk walking for 30 minutes on most days of the week.

What is Heart Disease?

Coronary heart disease (angina and heart attack) occurs when the coronary arteries become narrower or blocked due to ageing, poor diet and an unhealthy lifestyle. Tragically, the process can even begin in childhood. The narrowing of the arteries is due to fatty deposits forming in the smooth artery lining and is called atherosclerosis.

Angina

Narrowed coronary arteries reduce the rate at which blood can be delivered to the beating heart muscle. The muscle doesn't get enough oxygen to fuel the work it is doing and signals this with the pain of angina. Angina is usually felt across the front of the chest but sometimes in the shoulders, arms, throat or jaw. It is usually a heavy or tight pain, generally lasting less than ten minutes.

Heart Attack

A heart attack occurs when a coronary artery becomes entirely blocked due to the combination of atherosclerosis and the sudden development of a blood clot. The sudden blockage of the artery means that the part of the heart muscle that was supplied by that coronary artery is at once deprived of blood and oxygen. Muscle cannot survive without blood, so the affected area of the heart muscle dies and the pain is more intense and lasts longer than with angina.

Cholesterol

Cholesterol, a white waxy substance, is vital for the human body since it forms cell membranes, various hormones, bile salts and vitamin D. However, an excess of cholesterol in the blood can increase your risk of heart disease. A number of factors affect your blood cholesterol levels. Most cholesterol is made in the liver, but some is absorbed from food by the digestive system. Foods high in saturated fat, such as fatty meats, eggs, butter, cheese, whole milk, cream and cakes, increase your blood cholesterol levels.

Cholesterol travels to your body's cells through the bloodstream in tiny packages called lipoproteins. Scientists distinguish the types of packages by their density, and the most important types are low-density lipoprotein cholesterol (LDL cholesterol) and high-density

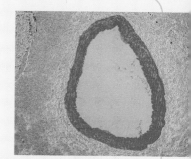

ABOVE: A healthy human coronary artery which is found on the surface of the heart and supplies blood to the heart muscle. The heart muscle is coloured blue in this example. The artery wall is coloured red.

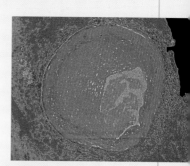

ABOVE: A blocked human artery. The coronary artery (coloured red) lies on the surface of the heart. The narrowed, light brown channel is blocked by a clot and the loss of blood supply to the heart muscle has resulted in a fatal heart attack.

ABOVE: Fruit and vegetables rich in antioxidant nutrients protect LDL cholesterol from oxidation.

Assessing and Reducing Risk Factors

There are a number of factors that influence the incidence of heart disease.

Factors That Can Be Reduced or Eliminated

High blood cholesterol levels

High blood pressure

Smoking

Diabetes

Being overweight

Lack of physical activity

Factors That You Cannot Change

♥ Age – the older you are, the greater the risk

♥ Gender – women before the menopause are at lower risk of heart disease than men

♥ Family history – you are at increased risk if there is heart disease in your family, especially in a close relative under 55

lipoprotein cholesterol (HDL cholesterol). Most of the blood cholesterol is carried as LDL cholesterol from the liver to other parts of the body.

Having a high level of LDL cholesterol increases your risk of heart disease because when oxidized it can slowly build up in the walls of coronary arteries and ultimately cause a heart attack. Therefore, your target level of LDL cholesterol should be below 3.0 mmol/l (195 md/dl).

HDL cholesterol acts as an arterial scavenger, carrying cholesterol away from body tissues, including artery walls, back to the liver. The higher the HDL cholesterol level, the lower your risk of heart disease. Your target level should be above 0.9 mmol/l (35 mg/dl).

High Blood Pressure

If your blood pressure is constantly above 140/90 mmHg, you have high blood pressure or hypertension. This adds to the workload of your heart and arteries. The heart must work harder than normal and this may cause it to enlarge. As you grow older your arteries will harden and become less elastic, and high blood pressure speeds up this process. It can be controlled by a combination of healthy eating, physical activity and medication.

People at Risk

People with diabetes are at high risk of heart disease and should pay particular attention to the risk factors, follow a healthy lifestyle and use appropriate drug therapy. Smoking cigarettes and other tobacco products also raises the risk of heart attack and stroke. Even passive smoking significantly increases the risk of heart disease.

Physical Activity

Physical activity helps prevent and treat heart disease as well as other major risk factors such as high blood pressure and high blood cholesterol. Medical studies have shown that just getting our bodies moving every day can have long-term health benefits.

The physical activity needs to be regular, of moderate intensity and aerobic. Aerobic exercise is any activity in which the large muscles in the arms or legs are moving rhythmically such as brisk walking, dancing or cycling. Even taking the stairs more often or parking your car further away from your destination can help increase your activity levels. Try to do at least 30 minutes of these activities on most days, and if you don't have 30 minutes to spare, try to do 15 minutes twice or ten minutes three times a day. Pick activities that are fun, that suit your needs and that you can do all year round.

The Disease–Diet Link

There is a wealth of information that links diet and the risk of heart disease. The emerging picture is that we should adopt a pattern of eating that can protect against heart disease. But there is no single individual dietary intervention that will guard you against heart disease, and you must look to make several changes to maximize the cardio-protective potential of what you eat.

The classic Seven Countries Study led by Ancel Keys in the 1960s showed a link between saturated fat intake and rate of heart disease in seven different countries. Keys showed that in Japan and the rural Mediterranean countries of southern Europe such as Greece and Italy, where the intake of saturated fat from meat and dairy products was low, there were significantly lower rates of heart disease than in the UK and the USA, where intakes of saturated fat were higher.

The Mediterranean Diet

The characteristic Mediterranean diet is high in fruit, vegetables, bread and other forms of cereals, potatoes, beans, nuts and seeds. It features olive oil as an important fat source, while dairy products, fish, poultry and eggs are consumed in low to moderate amounts. Little red meat is eaten, but a glass or two of wine compensates!

OLIVE OIL

Olive oil contains mainly monounsaturated fat (see page 13) and when used to replace saturated fat in the diet lowers total and LDL cholesterol without decreasing the 'good guy' HDL cholesterol. Substituting saturated fat with high levels of polyunsaturated fat or carbohydrates can produce the undesirable effect of decreasing HDL cholesterol.

FRUIT AND VEGETABLES

Another significant factor is that the Mediterranean-style diet is high in fruit and vegetables, which are rich in vitamins and minerals, essential fatty acids and antioxidants. There are about 600 antioxidants and these include the ACE vitamins, minerals and various other compounds that give fruit and vegetables their fabulous colours. Red wine and tea are also known to be good sources of antioxidants. The antioxidants protect LDL cholesterol from becoming oxidized, which makes it more toxic and more likely to accumulate in the artery walls. Fruit and vegetables also supply other protective nutrients. For example, folic acid is found in dark green vegetables, fruit and whole grains, and helps to maintain lower levels of homocysteine in the blood. High levels of homocysteine are linked to an increased risk of heart disease.

ABOVE: Mediterranean lifestyle has long been known to be healthy. We now know that an abundance of fresh fruit, vegetables and olive oil play a significant part.

The Lyon Diet Heart Study, carried out in France by A. Lorgeril *et al* and first published in 1994, provided evidence that if you adopt a Mediterranean-style diet after you have a heart attack, you can expect a dramatic reduction in the risk of another heart attack.

The Benefits of Soya Beans
In Asian countries, with traditionally high intakes of soya-bean products, there is far less cardiovascular disease. Soya beans contain phytoestrogens, naturally occurring compounds that are structurally similar to oestrogen. In addition, isoflavones in soya products exert a favourable effect on the lining of blood vessels and improve vascular tone.

The Benefits of Omega-3
Fish can play a huge part in preventing heart disease. People who eat fish and shellfish regularly, such as the Japanese and Greenland Inuits, have fewer heart attacks than non-fish eaters. Oily fish is the richest source of the polyunsaturated fatty acids – eicosapentanoic acid (EPA) and docosahexanoic Acid (DHA), or omega-3 fatty acids.

ABOVE: Countries that consume a lot of soya beans also have lower levels of cardiovascular disease due to the phytoestrogens in beans.

Omega-3 fatty acids are also found in seed oils, soya, nuts and green vegetables, and can play an important part in blood-clotting mechanisms, making the blood less sticky and reducing the risk of thrombosis.

Popping Pills Versus Real Food
Recent well-designed clinical trials (MRC/BHF Heart Protection Study, R. Collins, (UK), published 2002; GISSI study, R. Marchioli, (Italy), published 1999) have confirmed that there seems little benefit in taking individual nutrients such as vitamin E, C or beta-carotene in supplement form as vitamin preparations. This would suggest that the benefit may only occur when the antioxidants are taken as part of a healthy eating pattern, containing plenty of whole foods, including fruit and vegetables. However, if you can't eat fish, or don't like it, it is a good idea to take a supplement of omega-3 fatty acids (EPA and DHA) in capsule form, at 1 g per day.

Shaping Up
The shape you are has a link with heart disease. If you are apple-shaped, where fat is deposited around your stomach, you are at greater risk of heart disease than if you are pear-shaped, with fat distributed over your hips and thighs. This is because fat cells over the stomach make the body more resistant to the hormone insulin. To compensate, more insulin is produced, which increases blood pressure, cholesterol and triglycerides, lowers HDL cholesterol and increases the tendency for the blood to form clots. And of course your risk of becoming diabetic is increased. This clustering of risk factors is called the Insulin Resistance Syndrome.

By keeping to foods with a low glycaemic index (GI), you are less likely to develop insulin resistance, diabetes and heart disease. GI is a measurement of the effects of carbohydrate-rich foods on blood glucose levels. Starchy foods that take a long time to be digested and absorbed have a low GI, and have a favourable effect on blood glucose and insulin.

Top Ten Tips for Healthy Living

1 Enjoy a Wide Variety of Nutritious Foods

Eat a combination of different food, which will help give you all the essential nutrients in balanced proportions. Try to adopt the Mediterranean diet most of the time (see page 9). This should be a lifelong approach, not just a five-minute wonder, so make it easy for yourself by making simple changes one at a time. Above all, enjoy your food!

2 Be a Healthy Weight for Your Height

Make sure you keep to a healthy weight for your height by monitoring your waist measurement.

You should aim to keep your waist circumference in the healthy range – less than 93 cm (37 inches) for men and 80 cm (32 inches) for women. If your waist measurement is more than this, try to lose weight by reducing your energy intake to less than your body needs and increase your physical activity at the same time.

3 Eat Plenty of Fruit, Vegetables and Salad

You should eat at least five portions a day. An easy tip to remember is that a portion of fruit or vegetables is about the size of a clenched fist and that five portions should add up to 500 g (1 lb) in weight.

PORTION GUIDE

- ♥ 1 large fruit (such as an apple, orange or banana)
- ♥ 2 small fruits (such as plums or satsumas)
- ♥ 1 cup of raspberries, strawberries or grapes
- ♥ 1 glass (150 ml/¼ pint) of fruit juice
- ♥ 1 tablespoon of dried fruit
- ♥ 2 tablespoons of raw, cooked or frozen vegetables
- ♥ 1 dessert bowl of salad

4 Eat Fish Two or Three Times a Week

Eat more fish, particularly oily fish, especially if you have already had a heart attack. Oily fish are the richest source of omega-3 fatty acids. If you can't eat fish, you should take a daily

Waist Measurements

Men
93–100 cm (37–40 inches): you are overweight
Over 100 cm (40 inches): you are fat

Women
80–88 cm (32–35 inches): you are overweight
Over 88 cm (35 inches): you are fat

- ♥ Measure with a tape measure next to your skin, not over your clothes
- ♥ Make sure the tape is level at the navel
- ♥ Let the tape fit around your waist – don't pull too tightly
- ♥ Try to measure in the same place each time

supplement of 1 g of omega-3 fatty acids. Look out for a special variety of eggs that contain omega-3, produced by chickens that have been fed an omega-3-packed diet.

TOP FISH SOURCES OF OMEGA-3

	(omega-3 per portion)
Mackerel	4.5 g
Pilchards (canned in tomato sauce)	3.2 g
Trout	2.9 g
Salmon	2.5 g
Herring	2.2 g
Sardines (canned in tomato sauce)	2.0 g
Salmon (canned)	1.9 g
Crab (canned)	0.9 g

TOP PLANT SOURCES OF OMEGA-3

	(omega-3 per portion)
Flaxseed and flaxseed oil (linseeds and linseed oil)	1.8 g
Walnuts and walnut oil	1.5 g
Sweet potatoes and pumpkins	1.3 g
Rapeseed oil	1.1 g
Soya-bean oil	0.8 g
Spinach and leafy green vegetables	0.2 g

ABOVE: Stick to the advice in Tip 4 to ensure that your diet is getting an optimum amount of omega-3 fatty acids. If you do not eat fish, there are plenty of plant sources that will provide sufficient amounts as well.

5 Base Meals and Snacks Around Wholegrain Foods

Wholegrain foods include bread, cereals, rice, pasta and starchy food, such as potatoes. They are filling yet not fattening and are great sources of fibre, both soluble and insoluble.

♥ SOURCES OF FIBRE

Soluble – lowers cholesterol

Oats – rolled oats, oat bran, oat-based cereals and breads

Beans – peas, split peas, lentils, chickpeas, soya beans and baked beans

Some fruits – apples, strawberries and citrus fruits

Insoluble – prevents bowel problems

Wholegrain bread and cereals

Brown rice

Wholemeal pasta

Fruit and vegetables

6 Eat a Diet Low in Fat

There are three main types of fat in food – saturated, monounsaturated and polyunsaturated.

♥ SATURATED FATS
Found in: Fatty meats, full-cream dairy products such as milk, cream and cheese, coconut and palm oil used in convenience foods, cakes, pastries, biscuits, sweets, pre-packed foods and take-away meals.
Effect: Raise cholesterol

♥ TRANS FATS
Found in: Small amounts in the fat of dairy products and some meats but mainly in hydrogenated vegetable oils, some margarines and in commercially prepared foods such as biscuits, pastries, cakes, puddings and baked goods.
Effect: Raise cholesterol

ABOVE: If you want to use a spread, choose a low fat version made from vegetable oils that will help you to lower your cholesterol.

♥ POLYUNSATURATED FATS
Found in: Vegetable oils such as sunflower, corn, safflower, soya, grapeseed and nut oils and many margarines and spreads contain omega-6 polyunsaturated fatty acids. Vegetables and fish oils contain omega-3 fatty acids.
Effect: Lower cholesterol

♥ MONOUNSATURATED FATS
Found in: Olive and rapeseed (canola) oil, peanut oil and spreads, avocados and nuts.
Effect: Lower cholesterol

You should avoid saturated fat and choose fats that are unsaturated, particularly olive oil and rapeseed (canola) oil. Rapeseed oil is a good source of omega-3 fatty acids and is increasingly the chosen oil for most unspecified vegetable oils, but always check the label.

HOW MUCH FAT SHOULD YOU EAT IN A DAY?
A healthy fat intake is based on your energy needs and activity levels. An average man may require 2,500 kcals (calories) per day and an average woman 2,000 kcals per day. You need to limit

ABOVE: Experiment with the oil–water spray when griddling – try it on lean pork steaks for example, and accompany with steamed vegetables for an ultra healthy supper.

BELOW: Salt increases blood pressure so should definitely be kept out of any kitchen that is dedicated to a healthy heart diet.

your total fat intake so that around 35 per cent or less of your total calories come from fat.

If you need to lose weight, you should reduce your entire fat intake and this means even the good fats, since all fat is fattening! Use low-fat cooking methods such as microwaving, grilling, griddling, steaming, baking, casseroling and stewing.

DAILY GUIDELINES FOR FAT INTAKE

Intake in kilocalories (kilojoules)	Total fat in grams	Saturated fat in grams
1500 (6270)	57	15
1800 (7524)	68	18
2000 (8360)	70	23
2500 (10450)	95	32

COOKING THE OIL–WATER SPRAY WAY

You can reduce the fat in cooking by using an oil–water spray, which delivers far less oil than commercial oil sprays. Fill a small plastic spray bottle with seven-eighths water and one-eighth oil of your choice.

Use your oil–water spray when cooking under the grill, in a griddle pan, in a frying pan or in roasting pans before adding foods. Alternatively, actually spray the food for grilling, griddling, frying and roasting to give the lightest possible coating of oil. So don't brush – spray!

7 Choose Lean Meat, Poultry, Eggs, Beans, Nuts, Soya and Low-fat Dairy Foods

Eat a variety of protein foods – choose a different one each day. Pulses are good for your heart: peas, beans (including baked, kidney, soya, borlotti and butter beans), lentils and chickpeas are great sources of soluble fibre, which can help lower cholesterol. Soya protein also has a similar benefit. Nuts protect you from heart disease and you can eat up to four eggs a week.

8 Avoid Too Much Salt

Three-quarters of our salt intake now comes from salt added to processed food. So choose fresh foods rather than processed wherever possible, for example fresh meat and fish, fruit and vegetables.

💜 Avoid obviously salty foods – salted nuts, crisps, canned fish, ham, bacon, sausages, corned beef, canned foods, packet soups, commercial pies, cheeses and salad dressings.

💜 The easiest way to cut your salt intake is not to add it to food, either while cooking or at the table. Rock salt and sea salts are also sodium chloride and should be avoided. Replace the taste with fresh and dried herbs as well as other flavourings such as lemon juice, garlic, ginger and vinegars.

💜 Remember some foods that do not appear to be salty, such as bread and some cereals, do contain large quantities of salt. Again, check the label!

Units of Alcohol

1 unit of alcohol =
1 small beer, lager or cider
 (300 ml/1/2 pint)
1 small glass of red or
 white wine
 (125 ml/4 fl oz)
1 measure of spirits
 (25 ml/1 fl oz)
1 small glass of fortified wine,
 e.g. sherry, Martini
 (50 ml/2 fl oz)

9 Enjoy Alcohol With Your Food but be Sensible
If you like alcohol, then enjoy a unit or two each day with your meal. It is the pattern of drinking and the amount you consume that are the important factors rather than the type of drink. Avoid binge drinking and keep to safe levels of alcohol, with some alcohol-free days.

10 Try to Walk for Half an Hour Most Days
Eating for a healthy heart is part of a whole healthy lifestyle, which involves not smoking and being physically active. Brisk walking, cycling or climbing the stairs will benefit your heart. This will help you get fitter, control your weight and improve your HDL cholesterol. So keep moving!

LEFT: Don't worry if you do not enjoy exercise – try and find something active that you know you will be able to include in your day-to-day life. Even 'just walking' is perfectly suitable.

A Healthy Heart Diet

	Best Choice	In Moderation	Best Avoided
Cereals & Starchy Foods	Bread, chapattis, breakfast cereals, oats, porridge, rice, pasta, popcorn (without butter), all other cereals	Naan bread	Poppadoms (fried), waffles, croissants, Danish pastries, fried rice, noodles in cartons
Potatoes	Boiled, mashed, jacket, instant (without fat)	Oven chips, roast potatoes cooked in best-choice oil, fat-free crisps	Chips, potato croquettes, all other crisps
Vegetables & Fruit	A wide variety of vegetables, fruit, salads, pulses – raw (except for pulses), baked, boiled, steamed, and all fresh, frozen, dried, canned	Stir-fried vegetables in best-choice oils, coleslaw in homemade dressing, canned fruit in syrup	Ready-made coleslaw; vegetables in batter
Fish	White fish: cod, haddock, plaice, lemon sole, whiting; oily fish: mackerel, herring, salmon, tuna, trout; canned fish in water or tomato sauce: tuna, pilchards, sardines; shellfish: oysters, mussels, clams, whelks, winkles, scallops; squid	Canned fish in oil (drain or rinse off excess oil); fish in breadcrumbs; shellfish: shrimps, prawns, lobster, crab	Fried fish in batter: scampi, whitebait; roe, fish pâté, taramasalata
Meat	Well-trimmed grilled steak, chicken and turkey (with skin removed), venison, rabbit	Lean lamb, beef, pork; lean minced beef; grilled lean burgers; lean ham, gammon and lean bacon; liver and kidney; low-fat sausage	Fatty meats, crackling and skin; duck, sausages, sausagemeat, luncheon meat, corned beef, pâté, Scotch eggs, meat pies and pasties
Vegetarian Choices	Mycoprotein (Quorn), tofu, soya protein, pulses, chestnuts	All fresh nuts	Check fat content of vegetarian ready-made dishes

	Best Choice	In Moderation	Best Avoided
Eggs & Dairy	Egg white, skimmed milk, low-fat yogurt, very low-fat cheese: cottage cheese, fat-free fromage frais	Semi-skimmed, soya, goats', sheep's milk and their products; Greek yogurt, fromage frais, crème fraîche, evaporated milk; cheese: reduced-fat hard cheese, Edam, brie, camembert, feta, ricotta, mozzarella, cheese spread	Whole eggs (no more than four a week); whole milk, condensed milk, cream; cheese: Cheddar, Gouda, Gruyère, Roquefort, Stilton, cream cheese
Oils	Olive oil, rapeseed oil	Sunflower, corn, safflower, groundnut and sesame seed oils	Lard, suet, ghee and some vegetable oils, particularly palm and coconut oil
Spreads	Plant sterol or stanol spreads, low-fat spreads	Olive, rapeseed, sunflower and soya oil spreads	Butter, hard margarines
Whole Meals	Pasta with vegetable sauce, paella, kedgeree, kebabs skewered with best-choice ingredients, homemade soups	Homemade pizza, cottage pie, chilli con carne, fish pie, casseroles	Fish and chips, lasagne, pasta in cream sauce, pies, quiches, samosas, cream soups
Cakes & Biscuits	Homemade using best-choice ingredients; crispbreads, crumpets, rice cakes, matzos, breadsticks	Currant buns, scones, tea bread, malt loaf, fatless sponge; plain and semi-sweet biscuits, crackers	Cakes: ready-made, rich, sponge, fresh cream; doughnuts, pastries, chocolate biscuits
Puddings	Homemade using best-choice ingredients; meringue, low-fat milk puddings, jelly, sorbet	Frozen yogurt, ice cream, milk puddings, crumbles	Cheesecake, pastry, suet puddings
Flavourings, Sauces, Jams & Sweets	Pepper, herbs, spices, lemon juice, vinegar, garlic, tomato purée, mustard; homemade salad dressings and sauces made with best-choice ingredients; jam, marmalade, honey	Tomato ketchup, brown sauce, Worcestershire sauce, pickles, Bovril, Marmite, stock cubes, gravy granules, reduced-calorie mayonnaise and salad cream; hummus, peanut butter; mints and boiled sweets	Salt, salad cream, mayonnaise, cream sauces, ready-made cook-in sauces, chocolate spread, chocolates, toffees, fudge

Check the Label!

Label Checklist

Choose foods making
general claims such as:
- ❤ Healthy eating
- ❤ Diet, reduced-calorie or low-calorie
- ❤ Reduced-fat, low-fat or virtually fat-free
- ❤ Sugar-free
- ❤ Low-salt or reduced-salt

But beware:
- ❤ Some low-fat products may be full of sugar and therefore higher in calories than the standard product
- ❤ Cholesterol-free foods may still have plenty of fat and calories
- ❤ Sugar-free doesn't mean low-calorie or low-fat; such foods may be high in both

To help you make the right choices when buying food, always check the label. A lot of food eaten today is processed and it is sometimes difficult to know exactly what you are eating. Processed food has to have a label listing the main ingredients. The ingredients are always listed in order of weight, so that the main ingredient is first on the list.

Since you won't have time while shopping to read everything, here are some details that you can check at a glance.

Nutritional Information

Check the energy (kcals), fat and saturated fat per 100 g (3½ oz) or per serving. Compare similar products and choose the brand with the lowest figures. The fat content is probably the most useful piece of information.

UNDERSTANDING THE FAT CONTENT

The table opposite will help you to understand the details of fat content on food labels. In the example given here, the pizza contains nearly 20 g of fat and therefore one-third to one-fifth of the recommended fat for a day.

CHECKING PORTION SIZES

For meals and foods that you eat in large quantities, look at the amount per serving. For snacks and foods that you eat in small amounts, look at the 'per 100 g' information. Work out from the 'Ready reckoner' opposite whether there is a little or a lot of each nutrient in the food. Remember that the most important items to look for are calories, fat and sodium (salt).

CALCULATING THE SALT CONTENT

If you want to know the amount of salt (sodium chloride) in a product, multiply the sodium by 2.5 (1 g of sodium per 100 g (3½ oz) = 2.5 g salt per 100 g (3½ oz)). Try to keep your daily sodium intake to below 2.5 g = 2500 mg sodium = 6 g salt. In practice, this is hard to do since most of our daily intake comes from processed foods. As a general rule, reject any food that has more than 5 g fat per 100 g (3½ oz), especially when most of the fat is in the form of saturates. Choose oils and spreads that are rich in monounsaturates, and remember to avoid hydrogenated vegetable oil (trans fats).

Reading Labels

The example below shows you how to read a food label and get the information you need. Use it in conjunction with the nutritional information opposite and the Ready Reckoner below to make sure you know exactly what you are eating.

protein • measured in grams (g)
- most people eat more than enough protein so special guidelines aren't needed

carbohydrate • measured in grams (g)
- this includes sugars and starches
- it includes natural and added sugars
- 'of which sugars' is the amount of carbohydrate that comes from sugar

fibre • measured in grams (g)
- fibre is found in vegetables, fruit, beans and pulses
- the Guideline Daily Amounts (GDA) is 18 g for adults

sodium • measured in grams (g)
The Guideline Daily Amounts (GDA) is 2.5 g for adults

energy • measured in calories (kcal)
- the amount of energy that a food gives you
- the Guideline Daily Amounts is 2500 kcal (10,450 kJ) for men and 2000 kcal (8,360 kJ) for women

fat • measured in grams (g)
- the total amount of fat in the food
- includes saturates, polyunsaturates and monounsaturates
- eat less of all types especially saturates
- the Guideline Daily Amounts (GDA) is 95 g for men and 70 g for women

Tomato and Mozzarella Pizza

INGREDIENTS

Wheat flour, tomato (17%), water, mozzarella cheese (13%), olive oil, vegetable oil, yeast, oregano

NUTRITIONAL INFORMATION (typical values)

per 100g as consumed		per 150g (half pizza)
energy	229 kcals	344 kcal
	966 kJ	1445 kJ
protein	8.8 g	13.2 g
carbohydrate	33.6 g	50.4 g
fat	6.6 g	9.9 g
(of which saturates)	2.8 g	4.2 g
(monounsaturates)	2.6 g	4.0 g
(polyunsaturates)	1.2 g	1.7 g
fibre	2.0 g	3.0 g
sodium	2.7 g	4.1 g

'READY RECKONER' GUIDE TO FOOD LABELLING (figures per 100 g/3½ oz)

A lot		A little	
10 g of sugars		2 g of sugars	
20 g of fat		3 g of fat	
5 g saturated fat		1 g of saturated fat	
3 g of fibre		0.5 g of fibre	
500 mg sodium		100 mg of sodium	

Source: The British Heart Foundation

The Recipes

breakfasts

walnut & banana sunrise smoothie

Preparation time: 10 minutes **Serves 2**

NUTRITIONAL FACTS   ● kcals – 300 (1254 kJ)   ● Fat – 10 g, of which less than 1 g saturated   ● Sodium – 110 mg

1 Place all the ingredients in a food processor or blender and blend until smooth and frothy. Pour into 2 glasses.

OR YOU COULD TRY...
Your own mixture of delicious fresh fruits, prepare as necessary, then whiz them up with nothing more than a handful of crushed ice. Try a mixture of the following:
1 banana, 2 handfuls fresh or frozen blackberries, 1 handful chopped fresh pineapple, 150 ml (5 oz) natural yogurt, 150 ml (¼ pint) skimmed milk; or
2 handfuls fresh strawberries, 1 handful raspberries, 150 g (5 oz) strawberry soya yogurt, 150 ml (¼ pint) soya milk

1 orange, segmented
1 banana
150 ml (¼ pint) skimmed milk
150 g (5 oz) natural yogurt
25 g (1 oz) walnuts
3 teaspoons honey

NUTRITIONAL TIPS
Smoothies are a great way to increase your intake of soya protein. Use the recipe above with soya milk and a soya yogurt to give you 10 g of soya protein. There are 5 g of soya protein in each 150 ml (¼ pint) soya milk and each 150 g (5 oz) soya yogurt.

light 'n' low pancakes

Preparation time: 10 minutes, plus standing   **Serves 4**
Cooking time: 20 minutes
NUTRITIONAL FACTS* ○ kcals – 150 (630 kJ) ○ Fat – 3 g, of which less than 1 g saturated ○ Sodium – 60 mg

1 Sift the flour into a bowl. If using wholemeal flour, also add the bran left in the sieve to the flour in the bowl.

2 Beat the egg, milk and oil together, then slowly add to the flour. Stir the mixture until a smooth batter forms.

3 Leave to stand for about 20 minutes, then stir again.

4 Heat a little oil in a nonstick frying pan, or spray with an oil–water spray. When the oil is hot, add 2 tablespoons of the pancake mixture and shake the pan so that it spreads.

5 Cook the pancake for 2 minutes until the underside is lightly browned, then flip or turn over and cook the other side for a minute or so.

6 Keep the pancake warm in the oven while you cook the rest – you can stack one on top of the other as they are cooked. The mixture should make 8 pancakes in all. Serve with your chosen topping.

125 g (4 oz) brown or wholemeal
   plain flour
1 egg
300 ml (½ pint) skimmed milk
   (if using wholemeal flour you
   will need a little more)
1 teaspoon vegetable oil, plus
   a little extra for cooking, or
   use an oil–water spray (see
   page 14)

TOPPING IDEAS
chopped fresh fruit
chopped apple, raisins and
   ground cinnamon
cottage cheese
low-fat cream cheese
fruit spread or preserve

*figures per serving – 2 pancakes,
without topping

yogurt pots

Preparation time: less than 5 minutes   **Serves 1**

NUTRITIONAL FACTS*   O kcals – 84 (353 kJ)   O Fat – 2 g, of which less than 1 g saturated   O Sodium – 125 mg

1 Add one or more of the flavourings to the yogurt and stir to mix.

OR YOU COULD TRY...
Having fruit with your breakfast to start the day well. A one-portion 'fistful' of fruit contains less than 1 g of fat and no more than 100 calories. So choose from these two tropical fruit combinations (2 servings), preparing the fruit as necessary and mixing with the fresh fruit juice:
1 mango, 2 pineapple slices, 1 kiwi fruit, 250 ml (8 fl oz) pineapple juice; or 4 passion fruit, 2 slices of melon, 1 nectarine, 250 ml (8 fl oz) passion fruit juice or tropical fruit juice.

150 g (5 oz) natural yogurt or soya yogurt

FLAVOURING IDEAS
50 g (2 oz) rolled oats
3 tablespoons unsweetened breakfast cereal
1 tablespoon pine kernels, sunflower seeds or pumpkin seeds
1 tablespoon flaked almonds
1 tablespoon sultanas or raisins
1 piece fresh fruit, such as a chopped apple or sliced banana
50 g (2 oz) chopped fresh apricots or figs
1 small can peaches, pears or pineapple (in natural juice with no added sugar), drained and chopped
1 stewed or puréed apple with a sprinkling of ground cinnamon
50 g (2 oz) chopped dried fruit

*figures per 150 g (5 oz) carton of natural yogurt

creamy porridge with summer berries

Preparation time: 5 minutes

Cooking time: 10–20 minutes

Serves 2

NUTRITIONAL FACTS ● kcals – 280 (1176 kJ) ● Fat – 6 g of fat, of which less than 1 g saturated ● Sodium – 60 mg

1 Place the water and oats in a saucepan and bring to the boil. Simmer for 10–20 minutes, stirring occasionally.

2 Add the skimmed milk, stir and simmer for a few more minutes.

3 Serve with your chosen berries.

OR YOU COULD TRY...
Sweetening your porridge with these other fruity combinations:

● blueberries, loganberries, blackcurrants or redcurrants
● raisins and sultanas
● apricots and figs
● bananas and walnuts
● prunes and a little honey

600 ml (1 pint) water
125 g (4 oz) porridge oats
150 ml (¼ pint) skimmed milk
1 handful fresh, frozen and
   thawed, canned or cooked
   berries, such as raspberries,
   strawberries, blackberries
   or cranberries

NUTRITIONAL TIPS
Oats provide one of the richest sources of the dietary soluble fibre beta-glucan. The recommended intake for a cholesterol-lowering effect is 3 g of beta-glucan per day, which will reduce your total cholesterol by 0.2 mmol/l (6 mg/dl). This bowl of porridge would reduce your cholesterol by 0.1 mmol/l (4 mg/dl).

pumpkin seed & apricot muesli

Preparation time: 10 minutes   **Serves 2**

NUTRITIONAL FACTS   ○ kcals – 340 (1428 kJ)   ○ Fat – 12 g, of which 1 g saturated fat   ○ Sodium – 65 mg

1 Place the oats, sultanas or raisins, seeds, almonds and apricots in a bowl with the fruit juice or water.

2 Add the grated apple and stir to mix.

3 Top with skimmed milk, soya milk, natural yogurt or soya yogurt.

OR YOU COULD TRY...
A softer texture, by soaking the oats, sultanas and raisins with the fruit juice or water overnight.

50 g (2 oz) rolled jumbo oats
1 tablespoon sultanas or raisins
1 tablespoon pumpkin or
    sunflower seeds
1 tablespoon chopped almonds
25 g (1 oz) ready-to-eat dried
    apricots, chopped
2 tablespoons fruit juice, such as
    apple or orange juice, or
    water
2 small eating apples, peeled
    and grated
3 tablespoons skimmed milk,
    soya milk, natural yogurt or
    soya yogurt

NUTRITIONAL TIPS
Almonds and other nuts may help to lower your risk of heart disease. They are high in cardio-protective nutrients such as vitamin E, folate, magnesium, copper and arginine. Almonds are the richest nut source of vitamin E, one of the antioxidants believed to play a role in reducing the risk of heart disease by preventing the oxidation of LDL cholesterol.

smoked mackerel and chive pâté

Preparation time: 10 minutes	Serves 8

NUTRITIONAL FACTS   ○ kcals – 94 (395 kJ)   ○ Fat – 7 g, of which 1 g is saturated   ○ Sodium – 183 mg

1 Place the mackerel and cheese in a bowl and mash together well.

2 Add the remaining ingredients and mix well. Alternatively, mix all the ingredients together in a food processor or blender.

3 Spoon the mixture into 8 small individual serving dishes or 1 large serving dish or mould. Cover and refrigerate for at least 2 hours, or up to 4 hours. Serve the pâté chilled with Vegetable Batons (see page 30) and wholemeal toast, if liked.

OR YOU COULD TRY...
Using other omega-3-rich fish instead of mackerel in this recipe, such as canned (in water or brine), drained pilchards, salmon or tuna.

200 g (7 oz) smoked mackerel, skinned, boned and flaked
125 g (4 oz) low-fat soft cheese
1 bunch of chives, chopped
1 tablespoon fat-free vinaigrette
1 tablespoon lemon juice

NUTRITIONAL TIPS
Of all the oily fish which are readily available, mackerel is the richest source of omega-3 fatty acids, so enjoy it in all its many forms – fresh, canned or smoked. It is also one of the least expensive oily fish.

tahini hummus

Preparation time: 10 minutes Serves 6

NUTRITIONAL FACTS   ○ Kcals – 88 (370 kJ)   ○ Fat – 5 g, of which 0.6 g saturates   ○ Sodium – 93 mg

1 Place the chickpeas, tahini, garlic, lemon juice and cumin in a food processor or blender. Process until well blended, adding a little water or vegetable stock if you prefer a thinner consistency. Taste and add more garlic, lemon juice or cumin to your liking.

2 Transfer the hummus to a serving bowl. Sprinkle with paprika or chopped parsley. Serve with Vegetable Batons (see page 30) and Pitta Bread Crisps (see below) or Turkish bread. Or use as an alternative to spread on bread.

SERVE WITH...

Pitta bread crisps: cut a pitta bread, either wholemeal or white, into quarters or eighths. Split and separate each piece into two. Spread the pieces in a single layer on a nonstick baking sheet. Bake in a preheated oven, 150°C (300°F), Gas Mark 2, for 10–15 minutes, until the pieces of bread are dried out and crisp.

250 g (8 oz) canned chickpeas, rinsed and drained
2 tablespoons tahini (sesame seed paste)
3 garlic cloves, chopped
125 ml (4 fl oz) lemon juice
pinch of ground cumin
Vegetable Stock (see page 122) or water (optional)
paprika or chopped parsley, to garnish

red pepper & spring onion dip with vegetable batons

Preparation time: 10 minutes   V   **Serves 4**

Cooking time: 30–40 minutes

NUTRITIONAL FACTS*   ○ kcals – 60 (252 kJ)   ○ Fat – 1 g of fat, of which less than 0.5 g saturated   ○ Sodium – 2 mg

1 Slightly flatten the pepper quarters and place on a baking sheet. Wrap the garlic in foil and place on the sheet. Roast in a preheated oven, 220°C (425°F), Gas Mark 7, for 30–40 minutes until the pepper is slightly charred and the garlic is soft.

2 When cool enough to handle, remove the skin from the pepper and discard. Transfer the flesh to a bowl.

3 Squeeze the roasted garlic flesh from the cloves into the bowl.

4 Using a fork, roughly mash the pepper and garlic together. Stir in the soya yogurt and spring onions. Season to taste with pepper. Serve with the vegetable batons.

1 large red pepper, cut into
     quarters, cored and deseeded
2 garlic cloves, unpeeled
250 g (8 oz) soya yogurt
2 spring onions, finely chopped
freshly ground black pepper
selection of raw vegetables,
     such as carrots, cucumber,
     peppers, fennel, tomatoes,
     baby corn, mangetout, celery
     and courgettes, cut into
     batons, to serve

* figures for the dip only

NUTRITIONAL TIPS

This soya dip will provide you with 2 g soya protein. Research has shown that a daily intake of 25 g soya protein per day can significantly reduce total as well as LDL cholesterol (the 'bad guy') as part of a healthy diet.

spicy lentil & tomato soup

Preparation time: 20 minutes   (V)   **Serves 4**

Cooking time: 40–50 minutes

NUTRITIONAL FACTS   O kcals – 288 (1210 kJ)   O Fat – 2 g, of which less than 1 g saturated   O Sodium – 117 mg

1 Heat the oil in a large saucepan, add the onion, garlic and chilli (if using) and fry gently for 4–5 minutes until soft.

2 Add the lentils, bay leaf, celery, carrots, leek and stock. Cover and bring to the boil, then reduce the heat and simmer for 30–40 minutes until the lentils are soft. Remove the bay leaf.

3 Stir in the tomatoes, tomato purée, turmeric, ginger, coriander and pepper to taste. Allow to cool a little, then transfer to a food processor or blender. Process until smooth, adding more stock or water if necessary.

4 Reheat gently, before serving with a swirl of yogurt. Serve with crusty wholemeal bread, if liked.

1 tablespoon vegetable oil
1 large onion, finely chopped
2 garlic cloves, finely chopped
1 small green chilli, deseeded
  and finely chopped (optional)
250 g (8 oz) red lentils, washed
  and drained
1 bay leaf
3 celery sticks, thinly sliced
3 carrots, thinly sliced
1 leek, thinly sliced
1.5 litres (2½ pints) Vegetable
  Stock (see page 122)
400 g (13 oz) can chopped
  tomatoes
2 tablespoons tomato purée
½ teaspoon ground turmeric
½ teaspoon ground ginger
1 tablespoon chopped fresh
  coriander
freshly ground black pepper
natural yogurt, to garnish

NUTRITIONAL TIPS

All pulses – beans, peas and lentils – are high in soluble fibre, which is good for cholesterol reduction. They also make a soup satisfying, and this lentil soup is particularly filling!

sweet potato & butternut squash soup

Preparation time: 20 minutes

Cooking time: 30 minutes

 V

Serves 4

NUTRITIONAL FACTS ○ kcals – 260 (1092 kJ) ○ Fat – 6 g, of which less than 1 g saturated ○ Sodium – 206 mg

1 Heat the oil in a large saucepan and add the onion and garlic. Cover and cook very gently for 10 minutes, without colouring.

2 Add the spices, ginger, chilli, lime rind and honey and stir for 30 seconds, then add the sweet potato, squash, half the lime juice and the stock.

3 Cover and bring to the boil. Reduce the heat and simmer for about 10 minutes until the vegetables are almost tender. Stir in the chickpeas. Check the seasoning and add pepper to taste. Simmer for a further 10 minutes, then add the remaining lime juice to taste.

4 Allow to cool slightly, then process in a food processor or blender until very smooth, adding more stock if necessary to achieve the desired consistency. Reheat gently and stir in the fresh coriander just before serving.

1 tablespoon vegetable oil
1 onion, finely chopped
2 garlic cloves, finely chopped
1 teaspoon cumin seeds
1 teaspoon ground coriander
1 cm (½ inch) piece of fresh root
  ginger, peeled and finely
  grated
1 green chilli, deseeded and
  finely chopped
finely grated rind and juice of
  1 lime
1 teaspoon honey
375 g (12 oz) sweet potatoes,
  peeled and cut into small
  chunks
375 g (12 oz) butternut squash,
  peeled and cut into small
  chunks
1.2 litres (2 pints) Vegetable
  Stock (see page 122)
250 g (8 oz) canned chickpeas,
  rinsed and drained
handful of fresh coriander
  leaves, chopped

fennel & white bean soup

Preparation time: 15 minutes   (V)   **Serves 4**

Cooking time: 30 minutes

NUTRITIONAL FACTS   O kcals – 155 (657 kJ)   O Fat – 1 g, of which less than 1 g saturated   O Sodium – 550 mg

1 Place 300 ml (½ pint) of the stock in a large saucepan. Add the fennel, onion, courgette, carrot and garlic. Cover and bring to the boil. Continue boiling for 5 minutes, then remove the lid, reduce the heat and simmer gently for about 20 minutes until the vegetables are tender.

2 Stir in the tomatoes, beans and sage. Season to taste with pepper and pour in the remaining stock. Simmer for five minutes, then allow the soup to cool slightly.

3 Transfer 300 ml (½ pint) of the soup to a food processor or blender and process until smooth. Return the blended portion to the pan, stir and heat through gently.

900 ml (1½ pints) Vegetable
   Stock (see page 122)
2 fennel bulbs, trimmed and
   chopped
1 onion, chopped
1 courgette, chopped
1 carrot, chopped
2 garlic cloves, finely sliced
6 tomatoes, finely chopped, or
   400 g (13 oz) can tomatoes
2 x 400 g (13 oz) cans butter
   beans, rinsed and drained
2 tablespoons chopped sage
freshly ground black pepper

NUTRITIONAL TIPS

When buying canned vegetables, choose the 'no added salt' varieties. If these are not available, rinse and drain vegetables such as beans and sweetcorn. This removes some but not all of the salt.

speedy mediterranean pasta

Preparation time: 10 minutes
Cooking time: 20 minutes

(V)

Serves 4

N U T R I T I O N A L   F A C T S   O kcals – 305 (1281 kJ)   O Fat – 3 g, of which less than 1 g saturated fat   O Sodium – 54 mg

1 Place all the ingredients, except the pasta and Parmesan, in a saucepan and simmer, uncovered, for 15 minutes.

2 Meanwhile, cook the pasta according to the packet instructions until it is just tender.

3 Allow the sauce to cool a little, then transfer to a food processor or blender. Process until smooth.

4 Drain the pasta, return to the pan and toss with the sauce. Sprinkle with Parmesan, if liked, and serve with a green salad and French bread.

400 g (13 oz) can chopped
   tomatoes
1 onion, chopped
1 garlic clove, crushed
2 tablespoons chopped basil
1 teaspoon dried rosemary
1 glass red wine (optional)
375 g (12 oz) dried pasta
Parmesan cheese, to serve
   (optional)

OR YOU COULD TRY...
Adding some of the following to the sauce to vary the flavour:
O Freshly steamed vegetables
O Canned beans, rinsed and drained
O Tuna, rinsed and drained
O Pitted olives
O A handful of walnuts

crispy potato skins

Preparation time: 10 minutes

(V)

Serves 2

Cooking time: 1 hour 50 minutes

NUTRITIONAL FACTS ○ kcals – 115 (483 kJ) ○ Fat – less than 1 g, of which negligible saturated ○ Sodium – 10 mg

1 Scrub the potatoes and place in a preheated oven, 220°C (425°F), Gas Mark 7, for 1¼ hours until tender. Alternatively prick the potatoes and place on kitchen paper in the microwave and cook on maximum (100%) for 6 minutes, turn and cook for a further 7 minutes, or follow the instructions in your handbook.

2 Halve the potatoes, scoop out the insides, leaving a shell about 6 mm (¼ inch) thick. (Save the scooped-out potato for another use, such as for a root mash or in a soup.) Cut each of the shells in half lengthways.

3 Spray a nonstick baking sheet with oil–water spray. Place the potato quarters, skin side down, on the sheet and spray lightly with oil–water spray. Bake in a preheated oven, 200°C (400°F), Gas Mark 6, for 25–35 minutes until golden brown and very crisp. Serve immediately.

2 large baking potatoes

oil–water spray (see page 14)

OR YOU COULD TRY...

Them on their own with just a shower of black pepper and a squeeze of fresh lemon juice, with dips such as Tahini Hummus (see page 45), or Red Pepper and Spring Onion Dip (see page 46). Alternatively, they can also be served as a vegetable accompaniment to meat, poultry or fish dishes when you want a potato dish with a crisp texture.

NUTRITIONAL TIPS

By using the oil–water spray, these potato skins become a really low-fat snack compared to the conventional version which is usually topped with crispy bacon and cheese and smothered in sour cream.

garlic, pea & parmesan crostini

Preparation time: 25 minutes   **(V)**   **Serves 8**

Cooking time: 55 minutes

NUTRITIONAL FACTS   ○ kcals – 200 (840 kJ)   ○ Fat – 12 g, of which 2 g saturated   ○ Sodium – 228 mg

1 Roast the garlic following the method for Garlic Mash (see page 72).

2 Meanwhile, to make the crostini, cut the loaf into 40 slices about ½–1 cm (¼–½ inch) thick. Using an oil-water spray or pastry brush, lightly coat each side of the bread slices with oil.

3 Place the bread slices on a rack and bake in a preheated oven, 200°C (400°F), Gas Mark 6, for about 5–10 minutes, turning the bread over as it turns pale gold. Remove and allow to cool.

4 Cook the peas in boiling water until tender. Drain and transfer to a food processor or blender or mash in a bowl with a fork. Separate the garlic cloves, squeeze out the roasted garlic flesh and add to the peas with the spread and Parmesan. Process or mash to a creamy purée. Allow to cool before spreading on to the crostini. Garnish with parsley or mint, if liked.

1 head of garlic
1 French baguette
olive oil–water spray (see page 14) or a little olive oil
200 g (7 oz) frozen peas
1 tablespoon unsaturated spread
2 tablespoons freshly grated Parmesan cheese
1 tablespoon chopped mint
parsley to garnish

OTHER CROSTINI TOPPINGS
Reduced-fat soft cheese and prawns
Red or green pesto sauce
Green olive paste
Smoked Mackerel and Chive Pâté (see page 28)
Goats' cheese
Tahini Hummus (see page 29)

> NUTRITIONAL TIPS
> *Crostini, made with olive oil, follow the beneficial Mediterranean diet rule for a starter or snack. Olive oil is a rich source of monounsaturates and vitamin E. Add lots of vegetables to the toppings for extra antioxidant nutrients.*

mediterranean vegetable & walnut salad

Preparation time: 30 minutes **Serves 6**

NUTRITIONAL FACTS • kcals – 300 (1260 kJ) • Fat – 13 g, of which 1 g saturated • Sodium – 550 mg

1 Heat the walnuts in a dry pan over a medium heat for 1–2 minutes until slightly toasted.

2 Whisk together the olive vinaigrette and olives in a small bowl.

3 Mix together the chickpeas, pepper, carrot and onion in a medium bowl. Toss with 3 tablespoons of the vinaigrette.

4 Toss the spinach and other salad leaves with the remaining vinaigrette. Transfer to a large serving bowl, top with the vegetable mixture and sprinkle with walnuts.

75 g (3 oz) walnuts, chopped
75 ml (3 fl oz) Olive Vinaigrette
  (see page 123)
1 tablespoon pitted olives
400 g (13 oz) can chickpeas
1 red pepper, cored, deseeded
  and thinly sliced
1 large carrot, cut into
  matchsticks
1 small red onion, thinly sliced
4 handfuls of baby spinach
4 handfuls of green salad leaves

NUTRITIONAL TIPS
Walnuts are one of the richest plant sources of omega-3 fatty acids available. A handful of walnuts provides as much omega-3 as a 75 g (3 oz) portion of salmon. Walnut oil is also rich in omega-3.

oriental-style coleslaw

Preparation time: 20 minutes **Serves 6**

NUTRITIONAL FACTS ● kcals – 160 (672 kJ) ● Fat – 10 g, of which 1 g saturated ● Sodium – 35 mg

1 Place all the salad ingredients in a large serving bowl and toss them well to combine.

2 For the dressing, heat the sesame seeds in a small, dry saucepan over a medium heat, shaking the pan frequently for 2–3 minutes until toasted.

3 Stir in the remaining dressing ingredients. Remove the pan from the heat, immediately pour the dressing over the salad. Toss to combine.

OR YOU COULD TRY...
Varying the coleslaw recipe above by substituting or adding one or more of the following ingredients: white cabbage, fennel, celery, onions, apples, oranges, sunflower seeds, pumpkin seeds, dried fruit, such as sultanas, raisins and ready-to-eat apricots, walnuts, pine nuts, garlic, fresh herbs.

1 white radish, cut into long, thin strips
1 large carrot, cut into long, thin strips
½ Chinese cabbage, shredded
¼ red cabbage, shredded
2 spring onions, cut into long, thin strips
18 mangetout, cut lengthways into thin, strips
50 g (2 oz) spinach, shredded
50 g (2 oz) fresh or dried figs, cut lengthways into quarters
75 g (3 oz) flaked almonds

DRESSING
2 tablespoons sesame seeds
3 teaspoons grated fresh root ginger
1 teaspoon sugar
3 tablespoons sherry or rice wine vinegar
2 teaspoons peanut oil
2 teaspoons reduced-salt soy sauce
a few drops of sesame oil (optional)

baked beetroot, spinach & orange salad

Preparation time: 20 minutes   **V**   **Serves 4**
Cooking time: 1–2 hours

NUTRITIONAL FACTS   ◦ kcals – 125 (525 kJ)   ◦ Fat – 2 g, of which less than 1 g saturated   ◦ Sodium – 410 mg

1 To bake the beetroot, place the whole beetroots on a piece of foil large enough to enclose them loosely, spread with the garlic and oregano. Season to taste with pepper and drizzle over the oil and vinegar.

2 Gather up the foil loosely and fold over at the top to seal. Place on a baking sheet and bake in a preheated oven, 200°C (400°F), Gas Mark 6, for 1–2 hours, depending on size of the beetroot, until tender.

3 Remove from the oven and allow them to cool before peeling and slicing the beetroot. Discard the garlic.

4 Place the spinach in a layer in the bottom of a large salad bowl followed by alternate layers of beetroot and orange.

5 Drizzle over the dressing and season with pepper to taste. Garnish with oregano.

OR YOU COULD TRY...
The baked beetroot which is also delicious served hot as a vegetable accompaniment to meat and fish, or roughly mashed to a purée, in which case the baked garlic can be added to the mash.

500 g (1 lb) raw whole beetroots, preferably of even size
2 garlic cloves
handful of oregano leaves
1 teaspoon olive oil
1 tablespoon balsamic vinegar
200 g (7 oz) baby spinach
2 oranges, segmented
5 tablespoons Olive Vinaigrette (see page 123)
freshly ground black pepper
chopped oregano, to garnish

NUTRITIONAL TIPS
Beetroot is important for heart health as it contains a high amount of antioxidants, as indicated by its vibrant colour. It also contains other beneficial vitamins and minerals including beta-carotene, vitamins B6 and C, folic acid, manganese, calcium, magnesium, iron, potassium and phosphorous – all important for heart health.

tabbouleh

Preparation time: 15 minutes, plus standing Serves 6

NUTRITIONAL FACTS   ❍ kcals – 134 (563 kJ)   ❍ Fat – 22 g, of which a less than 1 g saturated   ❍ Sodium – 8 mg

1 Place the bulgar wheat in a bowl. Pour over boiling water to cover and leave to stand for 45–60 minutes until the grains swell and soften.

2 Drain and press to remove excess moisture. Place in a salad bowl. Add the onion, tomatoes, cucumber, parsley and mint. Toss to combine.

3 For the dressing, place the ingredients in a screw-top jar, replace the lid and shake well to combine. Pour over the salad and toss to coat. Cover and refrigerate until ready to use – within 2–3 days.

OR YOU COULD TRY...
Tabbouleh as an accompaniment for fish and meat dishes, such as Orange and Cider Poached Mackerel (see page 65), or Turkish Lamb and Potato Stew (see page 105). It is also tasty as a baked potato topping or as a filling for pitta bread.

175 g (6 oz) bulgar wheat
300 ml (½ pint) boiling water
1 red onion, finely chopped
3 tomatoes, diced
¼ cucumber, chopped
10 tablespoons chopped parsley
5 tablespoons chopped mint

DRESSING
100 ml (3½ fl oz) lemon juice
2 teaspoons olive oil
freshly ground black pepper

three bean & tuna salad

Preparation time: 15 minutes   **Serves 6**

Cooking time: 5 minutes

NUTRITIONAL FACTS   ❍ kcals – 130 (546 kJ)   ❍ Fat – 3 g, of which less than 1 g saturated   ❍ Sodium – 560 mg

1 If using fresh or frozen French beans, lightly cook for 4–5 minutes in boiling water, or steam or microwave. Refresh under cold running water, then drain well.

2 Flake the tuna and place in a bowl with all the beans and the onion.

3 Mix together the dressing ingredients and pour over the bean and tuna mixture.

4 Toss lightly and garnish with olives. Serve on a bed of salad leaves.

175 g (6 oz) French beans, canned, fresh or frozen
200 g (7 oz) can tuna, rinsed and drained
175 g (6 oz) canned butter beans, rinsed and drained
175 g (6 oz) canned red kidney beans, rinsed and drained
1 onion, finely sliced
12 olives, to garnish
salad leaves, to serve

DRESSING
1 teaspoon Dijon mustard
2 tablespoons balsamic vinegar
1 tablespoon olive oil
1 tablespoon tomato purée
1 small garlic clove, crushed
2 tablespoons chopped parsley
pinch of dried basil or oregano
freshly ground black pepper

NUTRITIONAL TIPS
The many beans in this dish are abundant in cardio-protective nutrients. Combined with low-fat canned tuna, this salad is a healthy complement to any meal.

orange & almond couscous salad

Preparation time: 15 minutes, plus standing

Cooking time: 5 minutes

Serves 6

NUTRITIONAL FACTS ❍ kcals – 160 (672 kJ) ❍ Fat – 4 g, of which 0.3 g saturated ❍ Sodium – 6 mg

1 Place the apple juice in a saucepan and bring to the boil. Slowly stir in the couscous. Remove the pan from heat. Cover and leave to stand for 10 minutes. Fluff up with a fork.

2 Add the pepper, herbs and currants to the couscous. Toss to combine. Transfer to a serving bowl. Scatter with the orange segments and onion.

3 For the dressing, place the ingredients in a small saucepan and heat gently to dissolve the honey – do not allow to boil. Drizzle over the salad. Scatter with the almonds.

250 ml (8 fl oz) apple juice
175 g (6 oz) couscous
½ red pepper, cored, deseeded
  and diced
4 tablespoons chopped parsley
3 tablespoons chopped mint
25 g (1 oz) currants
2 oranges, segmented
1 red onion, sliced
25 g (1 oz) flaked almonds

DRESSING
juice of 1 orange
juice of 1 lemon or lime
2 teaspoons olive or hazelnut oil
1 teaspoon honey

NUTRITIONAL TIPS
Almonds (see also the Nutritional Tip on page 26) contain the amino acid arginine (amongst other vital nutrients), which is thought to improve the health of artery linings and reduce the risk of heart disease.

caponata ratatouille

Preparation time: 20 minutes   **V**   **Serves 6**
Cooking time: 40 minutes

NUTRITIONAL FACTS   ◗ kcals – 90 (378 kJ)   ◗ Fat – 4 g, of which 1 g saturated   ◗ Sodium – 155 mg

1 Cut the aubergines and onions into 1 cm (½ inch) chunks.

2 Heat the oil in a nonstick frying pan until very hot, add the aubergine and fry for about 15 minutes until very soft. Add a little boiling water to prevent sticking if necessary.

3 Meanwhile, place the onion and celery in a saucepan with a little water or wine. Cook for 5 minutes until tender but still firm.

4 Add the tomatoes, thyme, cayenne pepper, aubergine and onions. Cook for 15 minutes, stirring occasionally.

5 Add the capers, olives, wine vinegar, sugar and cocoa powder (if using) and cook for 2–3 minutes. Season with pepper and serve garnished with almonds and parsley. Serve hot or cold as a side dish, starter or a main dish. Serve with polenta and hot crusty bread, if liked.

750 g (1½ lb) aubergines
1 large Spanish onion
1 tablespoon olive oil
3 celery sticks, coarsely chopped
a little wine (optional)
2 large beef tomatoes, skinned
    and deseeded
1 teaspoon chopped thyme
¼–½ teaspoon cayenne pepper
2 tablespoons capers
handful of pitted green olives
4 tablespoons wine vinegar
1 tablespoon sugar
1–2 tablespoons cocoa powder
    (optional)
freshly ground black pepper

TO GARNISH
toasted, chopped almonds
chopped parsley

NUTRITIONAL TIPS
Aubergines can absorb a lot of fat when fried and therefore it is important to measure the amount of olive oil and not be tempted to add any more. Instead of using oil, you can sauté vegetables in wine, water or stock with tasty results.

spicy pinto & borlotti beans in tomato sauce

Preparation time: 10 minutes

Cooking time: 20 minutes

Serves 4

NUTRITIONAL FACTS   ○ kcals – 170 (714 kJ)   ○ Fat – 1 g, of which less than 1 g saturated   ○ Sodium – 160 mg

1 Mix together the onions, garlic, chilli, spices and 300 ml (½ pint) of the stock in a frying pan. Cover and boil for 5 minutes. Uncover and simmer briskly for about 5 minutes until the onions are tender and the liquid has almost gone.

2 Stir in the remaining stock, beans and passata. Simmer, partially covered, for about 10 minutes until thick.

3 Stir in the lime juice and herbs. Season to taste with pepper. This dish can be used as an alternative to refried beans as part of a Mexican meal. You can use any canned beans but the borlotti and pinto beans give a lovely pink colour to this dish.

2 onions, chopped
4 garlic cloves, crushed
1 chilli, deseeded and chopped
1 tablespoon ground cumin
½ tablespoon ground coriander
375 ml (13 fl oz) Vegetable Stock
    (see page 122)
300 g (10 oz) can pinto beans,
    rinsed and drained
300 g (10 oz) can borlotti beans,
    rinsed and drained
300 ml (½ pint) passata
juice of 1 lime
2 tablespoons each chopped
    parsley, mint and coriander
freshly ground black pepper

NUTRITIONAL TIPS
While pulse protein is valuable, it can be made more so by combining it with protein from cereal foods. This nutritional principle may not be familiar to you, but the practical examples certainly will be – baked beans on toast, lentil soup with bread, Indian dhal with rice or chapattis, and spicy beans with tortillas.

mushroom & pea bhaji

Preparation time: 10 minutes   (V)   **Serves 4**

Cooking time: 20 minutes

NUTRITIONAL FACTS   ● kcals – 90 (378 kJ)   ● Fat – 4 g, of which 0.5 g saturated   ● Sodium – 15 mg

1 Heat the oil in a saucepan, add the onion and fry gently for 2–3 minutes until it begins to soften. Add the cumin and mustard seeds and fry, stirring, for another 2 minutes.

2 Add the tomatoes, chilli, mushrooms and peas. Stir and cook for 2 minutes.

3 Add the chilli powder and turmeric, mix well, then cook, uncovered, for a further 5–7 minutes.

4 Add the pepper, garlic and coriander leaves and cook for 5 minutes until the mixture is quite dry. Garnish with the spring onion or chives. Serve as a vegetable accompaniment to Tandoori Chicken (see page 104) or Kofta Curry (see page 106), if liked.

2 tablespoons vegetable oil
50 g (2 oz) onion, finely sliced
1/4 teaspoon cumin seeds, crushed
1/4 teaspoon mustard seeds
125 g (4 oz) tomatoes, chopped
1 green chilli, deseeded and finely chopped
425 g (14 oz) button mushrooms, halved (or quartered if larger)
150 g (5 oz) frozen peas
1/2 teaspoon chilli powder
1/4 teaspoon turmeric
1 red pepper, cored, deseeded and chopped
4 garlic cloves, crushed
2 tablespoons fresh coriander leaves
chopped spring onions or chives, to garnish

spiced roast roots

Preparation time: 20 minutes   **Serves 6**

Cooking time: 40 minutes

NUTRITIONAL FACTS   O kcals – 100 (420 kJ)   O Fat – 3 g, of which less than 1 g saturated   O Sodium – 30 mg

1 Place all the vegetables and garlic in a large roasting tin. Sprinkle over the crushed seeds and squeeze over the ginger pulp to extract the juice. Season to taste with pepper and drizzle over the oil.

2 Roast in a preheated oven, 200°C (400°F), Gas Mark 6, for 30 minutes, turning occasionally.

3 Pour over the wine and return to the oven for a further 10 minutes. Garnish with parsley. Serve as a side dish or as a main meal, with fresh baked bread toasted with a topping of reduced-fat cheese.

4 carrots, thickly sliced diagonally

250 g (8 oz) swede, cubed

250 g (8 oz) sweet potato, cubed

1 onion, cut into 8 wedges

2 leeks, thickly sliced diagonally

6 garlic cloves

½ teaspoon mustard or cumin seeds, lightly crushed

½ teaspoon coriander seeds, lightly crushed

2 cm (1 inch) piece fresh root ginger, peeled and finely grated

1 tablespoon olive oil

100 ml (3½ fl oz) dry white wine

freshly ground black pepper

1 tablespoon flat leaf parsley, to garnish

NUTRITIONAL TIPS
Garlic is thought to be good for your heart but not enough scientific trials have yet been carried out to confirm the benefits. It certainly contains a substance called allicin, which dilates the blood vessels and reduces blood clotting.

speedy vegetable stir-fry

Preparation time: 10 minutes

Cooking time: 10 minutes

(V)   **Serves 6**

N U T R I T I O N A L   F A C T S   ○ kcals – 300 (1260 kJ)   ○ Fat – 12 g, of which 2 g saturated   ○ Sodium – 775 mg

1 Prepare the noodles according to the packet instructions.

2 Meanwhile, heat the oil to a high heat in a wok or frying pan . Add the baby corn, mangetout and pepper and stir-fry for 2 minutes. Then add the baby spinach or other leafy green vegetable, shallot, garlic and ginger and stir-fry for another 1–2 minutes.

3 Drain the noodles and add them to the pan. Stir-fry for 1 minute. Drizzle with sauce to taste before serving.

75 g (3 oz) fresh rice or fine egg
noodles
handful each of baby corn,
mangetout, baby spinach or
other leafy green vegetable
½ red pepper, cored, deseeded
and cut into fine strips
1 shallot, finely chopped
1 garlic clove, chopped
2 cm (1 inch) piece fresh root
ginger, peeled and grated
2 teaspoons Teriyaki Sauce (see
page 124) or oyster sauce
2 teaspoons sesame oil

N U T R I T I O N A L   T I P S
*Stir-frying is a quick and healthy
method of cooking. You should
use only a small amount of oil
and cook the food quickly to
retain all the nutrients. The oil
should be very hot, to seal the
food and limit the absorption
of fat. Do not be tempted to
add extra oil when stir-frying to
prevent the food from sticking.
Remember that you can also
stir-fry with water, wine, sherry
or stock.*

thai-style monkfish & mushroom kebabs

Preparation time: 15 minutes, plus marinating	**Serves 4**

Cooking time: 10 minutes

NUTRITIONAL FACTS ○ kcals – 192 (806 kJ) ○ Fat – 5 g, of which less than 1 g saturated ○ Sodium – 34 mg

1 Combine the ingredients for the marinade in a large bowl. Cut the fish into large cubes and add to the marinade with the onion, mushrooms and courgette. Cover and refrigerate for 1 hour to allow the flavours to blend.

2 Brush the rack of a grill pan lightly with oil to prevent the kebabs from sticking. Thread 4 skewers with alternate chunks of fish, mushrooms, courgette and onion. Brush with a little oil and grill under a preheated hot grill for about 10 minutes, turning at intervals. Garnish with watercress or flat leaf parsley.

OR YOU COULD TRY...
Any firm white fish such as halibut, sea bass, swordfish, cod or haddock, if you prefer.

500 g–750 g (1–1½ lb) monkfish
   tails, skinned
1 onion, quartered and layers
   separated
8 mushrooms
1 courgette, cut into 8 pieces
vegetable oil, for brushing
watercress or flat leaf parsley,
   to garnish

MARINADE
grated rind and juice of 2 limes
1 garlic clove, finely chopped
2 tablespoons finely sliced fresh
   root ginger
2 fresh chillies, red or green or
   1 of each, deseeded and finely
   chopped
2 lemon grass stalks, finely
   chopped
handful of chopped fresh
   coriander
1 glass red wine
2 tablespoons sesame oil
freshly ground black pepper

crab & coriander cakes

Preparation time: 25–30 minutes   **Serves 6**
Cooking time: 10 minutes
NUTRITIONAL FACTS   ○ kcals – 185 (777 kJ) ○ Fat – 5 g, of which 1 g saturated ○ Sodium – 509 mg

1 In a large bowl, mix together the crab meat, mashed potatoes, coriander, spring onions, lemon rind and juice, and half the beaten egg to bind.

2 Form the mixture into 12 cakes about 1 cm (½ inch) thick. Coat the cakes with flour, then dip into the remaining egg and then the breadcrumbs.

3 Heat the oil in a nonstick frying pan and fry the cakes for about 10 minutes until golden, turning once or twice.

4 Drain on kitchen paper before serving. Serve with a sweet red chilli sauce, or Tomato Salsa (see page 125).

OR YOU COULD TRY...
Using canned tuna or salmon, or fresh fish, and adding peas or sweetcorn. Try making a vegetable version using peas, broccoli and carrots instead of fish.

375 g (12 oz) canned crab meat, drained
250 g (8 oz) cold mashed potatoes
2 tablespoons chopped fresh coriander
1 bunch of spring onions, finely sliced
grated rind and juice of ½ lemon
2 eggs, beaten
flour, for coating
150 g (5 oz) fresh white breadcrumbs
1 tablespoon oil

NUTRITIONAL TIPS
Canned crab meat contains a moderate amount of omega-3 fatty acids (0.91 g omega-3 per 100 g). Canned fish is saltier than fresh fish (unless it is canned in water), so lower the salt content by putting the fish in a sieve or colander and rinsing it under cold running water. Drain thoroughly on kitchen paper.

parsley & garlic marinated sardines

Preparation time: 10 minutes

Serves 6

Cooking time: 5 minutes

NUTRITIONAL FACTS ● kcals – 180 (756 kJ) ● Fat – 10 g, of which 2.5g saturated ● Sodium – 112 mg

1 Place all the ingredients for the marinade in a small saucepan. Bring to the boil, then remove from the heat.

2 Place the sardines on a prepared barbecue or on a preheated hot griddle or under a hot grill. Cook for 1–2 minutes on each side until crisp and golden.

3 Place the sardines in a single layer in a shallow dish. Pour the dressing over the sardines and serve hot. Alternatively, cover and refrigerate for at least 1 hour before serving cold. Serve with Tabbouleh (see page 44) and a mixed green leaf salad, if liked.

OR YOU COULD TRY...
Draining a can of sardines and place in a food processor with 1 crushed garlic clove, 1 tablespoon drained capers, 6 pitted olives, some chopped parsley and 1 tablespoon of wine or balsamic vinegar. Process until blended. Spread on piping hot toast for a delicious snack or starter.

12 fresh sardines, cleaned, or use
    fillets if preferred

MARINADE
50 g (2 oz) chopped parsley
1 teaspoon freshly ground
    black pepper
1 garlic clove, crushed
finely grated rind and juice of
    1 lemon
2 tablespoons white wine
1 tablespoon olive oil

NUTRITIONAL TIPS
A 100 g (3½ oz) portion of fresh sardines contains 2.7 g of omega-3 fatty acids. This Mediterranean recipe is equally suitable for other types of fish that are high in omega-3 fatty acids (see page 12), such as mackerel and salmon.

puy lentils with flaked salmon & dill

Preparation time: 30 minutes   **Serves 4**
Cooking time: 45 minutes
NUTRITIONAL FACTS   ❍ kcals – 450 (1890 kJ)   ❍ Fat – 18 g, of which 3 g saturated   ❍ Sodium – 70 mg

1 Place the salmon on a sheet of foil and spoon over the wine. Gather up the foil and fold over at the top to seal. Place on a baking sheet and bake in a preheated oven, 200°C (400°F), Gas Mark 6, for 15–20 minutes until cooked. Allow to cool, then flake, cover and chill.

2 Flatten the pepper halves slightly. Grill skin side up under a preheated hot grill until charred. Enclose in a plastic bag for a few minutes. Remove from the bag, peel away the skin and cut the flesh into 2.5 cm (1 inch) cubes, reserving any juices.

3 Place all the dressing ingredients, except the oil, in a food processor or blender and process until smooth. Whilst processing, drizzle in the oil until the mixture is thick.

4 Place the lentils in a large saucepan with plenty of water, bring to the boil, then simmer gently for about 15–20 minutes until cooked but still firm to the bite. Drain and place in a bowl with the pepper, dill, most of the spring onions and pepper to taste.

5 Stir the dressing into the hot lentils and allow to infuse. To serve, top the lentils with the flaked salmon and gently mix through the lentils and dressing, squeeze over a little lemon juice and scatter over the remaining spring onions.

500 g (1 lb) salmon tail fillet
2 tablespoons dry white wine
4 red peppers, halved, cored and
    deseeded
175 g (6 oz) Puy lentils, well
    rinsed
large handful of dill, chopped
1 bunch of spring onions, finely
    sliced
lemon juice, for squeezing
freshly ground black pepper

DRESSING
2 garlic cloves
large handful of flat leaf parsley,
    chopped
large handful of dill, chopped
1 teaspoon Dijon mustard
2 green chillies, deseeded and
    chopped
juice of 2 large lemons
1 tablespoon extra virgin
    olive oil

chilli & coriander fish parcels

Preparation time: 15 minutes, plus marinating   **Serves 1**
Cooking time: 15 minutes
NUTRITIONAL FACTS   ❍ kcals – 127 (533 kJ)   ❍ Fat – 1 g, of which 0.2g saturated   ❍ Sodium – 90 mg

1 Place the fish in a non-metallic dish and sprinkle with lemon juice. Cover and leave in the refrigerator to marinate for 15–20 minutes.

2 Place the coriander, garlic and chilli in a food processor or blender and process until the mixture forms a paste. Add the sugar and yogurt and briefly process to blend.

3 Place the fish on a sheet of foil. Coat the fish on both sides with the paste. Gather up the foil loosely and turn over at the top to seal. Return to the refrigerator for at least 1 hour.

4 Place the parcel on a baking tray and bake in a preheated oven, 200°C (400°F), Gas Mark 6, for about 15 minutes until the fish is just cooked.

OR YOU COULD TRY...
Combining, for example, chicken, steak or salmon with your favourite vegetables and herbs and bake in foil to provide a flavourful dish complete with its own homemade sauce.

125 g (4 oz) cod, coley or haddock fillet
2 teaspoons lemon juice
1 tablespoon fresh coriander leaves
1 garlic clove
1 green chilli, deseeded and chopped
1/4 teaspoon sugar
2 teaspoons natural yogurt

NUTRITIONAL TIPS
Cod is a low-fat white fish, a good source of protein and a useful source of iron. It has only 0.3 g omega-3 fatty acids per 125 g (4 oz) portion, but nevertheless will still make a contribution to your omega-3 intake. People who eat fish regularly are less likely to die of heart disease than those who rarely or never eat it.

tuna & mixed vegetable pasta bake

Preparation time: 10 minutes
Cooking time: 30 minutes

Serves 4

NUTRITIONAL FACTS   ○ kcals – 400 (1680 kJ) ○ Fat – 6 g, of which 1 g saturated ○ Sodium – 425 mg

1 Heat the oil in a nonstick frying pan, add the onion and fry for about 5 minutes until soft.

2 Meanwhile, cook the macaroni according to the packet instructions, until just tender. Drain.

3 Mix the pasta with the onion, tuna, tomatoes, vegetables, cottage cheese and fromage frais or yogurt. Pour into a greased casserole or ovenproof dish. Top with the breadcrumbs.

4 Bake in a preheated oven, 180°C (350°F), Gas Mark 4, for about 30 minutes until golden on top. Serve with a mixed salad and Potato & Olive Bread (see page 70), if liked.

1 tablespoon vegetable oil
1 onion, chopped
250 g (8 oz) wholemeal macaroni
200 g (7 oz) can tuna, well drained and flaked
400 g (13 oz) can tomatoes
125 g (4 oz) cooked mixed frozen vegetables
125 g (4 oz) cottage cheese with chives
2 tablespoons natural fromage frais or yogurt
75 g (3 oz) wholemeal breadcrumbs

NUTRITIONAL TIPS
Canned tuna contains fewer omega-3 fatty acids than fresh tuna and other canned forms of oily fish because much of the fat is lost when it is pre-cooked before canning. This does not happen to the more oil-rich salmon, mackerel, sardines or pilchards. Nevertheless, canned tuna is a very useful low-fat and low-calorie fish, to keep in your store cupboard.

griddled honey-glazed tuna with parsnip purée

Preparation time: 15 minutes   **Serves 4**
Cooking time: 15 minutes
NUTRITIONAL FACTS   ○ kcals – 310 (1302 kJ)   ○ Fat – 10 g, of which 2 g saturated   ○ Sodium – 300 mg

1 Place the ingredients for the glaze in a small saucepan. Bring to the boil, then reduce the heat and simmer until the mixture reduces and is of a glaze consistency. Keep hot.

2 For the parsnip purée, steam the parsnips and potatoes until tender. Drain if necessary and place in a food processor or blender with the yogurt, horseradish (if using) and pepper to taste. Process until blended. Keep warm or reheat prior to serving.

3 Brush the tuna with oil. Cook on a preheated, very hot griddle or barbecue, or in a frying pan or under a grill, for 1–2 minutes. Turn and spoon the glaze over the tuna. Cook for a further 1–2 minutes – it is best if moist and still slightly pink in the centre.

4 To serve, top a mound of the purée with a tuna steak and spoon over the remaining glaze. Accompany with steamed green vegetables, if liked.

4 tuna steaks, about 125 g (4 oz) each
2 teaspoons olive oil

GLAZE
1 tablespoon honey
2 tablespoons wholegrain mustard
1 teaspoon tomato purée
2 tablespoons orange juice
1 tablespoon red wine vinegar or balsamic vinegar
freshly ground black pepper

PARSNIP PURÉE
2 parsnips, cut into chunks
2 potatoes, cut into chunks
50 g (2 oz) natural yogurt
2 teaspoons horseradish relish (optional)

NUTRITIONAL TIPS
Griddling is a healthy way to cook, since it requires little or no added fat, and any fat from the food can drain away. Griddle pans can be heated to a very high heat, which gives food a delicious flavour and helps to seal in all the juices.

cod with chilli butter beans & tomatoes

Preparation time: 15 minutes

Cooking time: 20 minutes

Serves 4

NUTRITIONAL FACTS   ○ kcals – 221 (930 kJ)   ○ Fat – 3 g, of which 0.5 g saturated   ○ Sodium – 408 mg

1 Heat the oil in a nonstick saucepan and add the celery, onion and garlic. Cook for about 5 minutes until softened. Add the tomatoes, tomato purée, beans and chilli. Simmer, uncovered, for 10 minutes.

2 Meanwhile, heat the wine in a separate saucepan. Add the fish and poach gently for about 3–4 minutes until just cooked through.

3 Combine the undrained fish with the bean and tomato mixture and heat through. Add pepper to taste and garnish with parsley. Serve with new potatoes, basmati rice or pasta and spinach or broccoli for a feast of colour.

2 teaspoons vegetable oil
1 celery stick, finely diced
1 onion, finely chopped
1 garlic clove, crushed, or 1 teaspoon minced garlic
400 g (13 oz) can tomatoes, undrained and mashed
2 tablespoons tomato purée
300 g (10 oz) can butter beans, well drained
1 green chilli, deseeded and finely chopped
125 ml (4 fl oz) dry white wine
500 g (1 lb) cod fillet (or any boneless white fish fillets), cut into cubes
freshly ground black pepper
2 tablespoons chopped parsley, to garnish

NUTRITIONAL TIPS
White fish such as cod, haddock, plaice and sole, for example, are all low in calories, low in fat and saturated fat and high in protein, minerals and vitamins. So, although they are low in omega-3 fatty acids, they are to be valued just as much as oily fish to help you beat heart disease.

orange & cider poached mackerel

Preparation time: 15 minutes
Cooking time: 10 minutes

Serves 4

NUTRITIONAL FACTS   ○ kcals – 208 (875 kJ)   ○ Fat – 4 g, of which 1 g saturated   ○ Sodium – 144 mg

1 Heat the oil in a large nonstick saucepan, add the pepper, spring onions and ginger and cook, stirring, for 1–2 minutes. Stir in the orange rind, cider, orange and lemon juices and soy sauce. Bring to the boil.

2 Reduce the heat and add the fish. Cover and cook for 5 minutes until the fish starts to flake when tested with a fork. Using a fish slice or slotted spoon, remove the fish from the cooking liquid and place on a plate. Cover with foil. Keep warm in the oven.

3 Add the coriander and pepper to the cooking liquid to taste. Bring to the boil. Boil rapidly until the mixture reduces to a sauce consistency. Serve with Tabbouleh (see page 44) or Baked Beetroot, Spinach & Orange Salad (see page 42), if liked.

1 teaspoon olive oil
1 red pepper, cored, deseeded
  and finely diced
2 spring onions, sliced
2.5–5cm (1–2 inch) piece of
  fresh root ginger, peeled
  and thinly sliced
1 teaspoon grated orange rind
125 ml (4 fl oz) dry cider
125 ml (4 fl oz) orange juice
2 tablespoons lemon juice
1 teaspoon reduced-salt soy
  sauce
4 mackerel fillets, about 150 g
  (5 oz) each, skinned
2 tablespoons chopped fresh
  coriander leaves
freshly ground black pepper

NUTRITIONAL TIPS
*Keep a good supply of frozen
fish, and other frozen food, in
the freezer. They are just as
nutritious as fresh foods in
some cases and can act as the
perfect healthy eating,
convenient way to cook your
evening meal.*

sea bass with mushroom & mixed herb stuffing

Preparation time: 15 minutes

Cooking time: 40 minutes

Serves 2

NUTRITIONAL FACTS   ○ kcals – 310 (1200 kJ)   ○ Fat – 9 g, of which 1.5 g saturated   ○ Sodium – 105 mg

1 Heat 1 teaspoon of the oil in a nonstick frying pan and gently cook the mushrooms for about 5 minutes until tender. Season to taste. Remove the pan from the heat and add the lemon rind and juice and herbs.

2 Meanwhile, cook the potatoes in boiling water or a steamer for about 10 minutes until just tender. Drain and allow to cool. Place the potatoes and garlic in a roasting tin, brush with most of the remaining oil and roast in a preheated oven, 200°C (400°F), Gas Mark 6, for about 20 minutes, until golden brown.

3 Make a crisscross incision on the skin side of the fish (to prevent the fish from curling). Make a cut lengthways down the side of each fillet into the centre and prise open creating a pocket for the stuffing. Brush with the remaining oil and stuff with the mushroom and herb mixture. Close the pocket to return the fish to its original shape.

4 Season with pepper to taste and place on top of the potatoes. Return to the oven and bake for 5–6 minutes (depending on size) until cooked through.

5 Serve with the fish placed on top of the potatoes and garnished with chopped herbs.

1 tablespoon olive oil
125 g (4 oz) mixed mushrooms, preferably wild, sliced
grated rind and juice of 1 lemon
handful of mixed herbs (such as flat leaf parsley, thyme, green or purple basil), roughly chopped
14 tiny new potatoes
1 garlic clove, crushed
2 sea bass fillets, about 125 g (4 oz) each
freshly ground black pepper
chopped herbs, to garnish

NUTRITIONAL TIPS
Sea bass contains a moderate amount of omega-3 fatty acids at 0.4 g per serving (100 g/ 3½ oz). The recommended amount is 1 g per day. You can add a further 0.9 g of omega-3 to your meal by serving spinach with your fish. Spinach contains 0.9 g omega-3 fatty acids per 100 g (3½ oz).

creamy kedgeree with peas

Preparation time: 15 minutes

Cooking time: 15 minutes

NUTRITIONAL FACTS   ◐ kcals – 460 (1932 kJ)   ◐ Fat – 8 g, of which 2 g saturated   ◐ Sodium – 672 mg

Serves 4

1 Cook the rice following the instructions on the packet. Place in a warmed serving dish.

2 Meanwhile, poach the fish in the milk in a saucepan for about 5 minutes until just cooked. Strain, reserving the cooking liquid. Skin and flake the fish, removing any stray bones, and set aside.

3 In a separate small saucepan, heat the oil and add the spring onions and curry paste. Cook gently for about 5 minutes until soft.

4 Combine the fish, rice, spring onion mixture, peas and chopped eggs in a large saucepan. Heat through, adding a little of the reserved cooking liquid if necessary. Season to taste with pepper.

5 Serve, garnished with tomatoes, parsley and lemon wedges.

250 g (8 oz) basmati rice
250 g (8 oz) haddock or any white fish
250 g (8 oz) smoked haddock
450 ml (³⁄₄ pint) semi-skimmed milk
1 teaspoon olive oil
2 spring onions, chopped
2 teaspoons curry paste
125 g (4 oz) frozen peas, cooked
2 hard-boiled eggs, shelled and chopped
freshly ground black pepper

TO GARNISH
chopped tomatoes
chopped parsley
lemon wedges

NUTRITIONAL TIPS
Basmati rice has the lowest glycaemic index (GI) of any rice. The GI of rice depends upon its amylose content – a type of starch that is broken down and absorbed relatively slowly by the body.

fisherman's pie with fresh spinach

Preparation time: 15 minutes | Serves 4
Cooking time: 40 minutes
NUTRITIONAL FACTS ● kcals – 360 (1512 kJ) ● Fat – 11 g, of which 2 g saturated ● Sodium – 822 mg

1 In a large saucepan, poach the fish in the milk with the bay leaf for 10 minutes until tender. Strain, retaining the cooking liquid. Skin and flake the fish, removing any stray bones, and set aside.

2 Meanwhile, heat the oil in a small saucepan, add the onion and carrot and cook gently for about 4 minutes. Steam the spinach and squeeze out any excess moisture.

3 Pour the fish-cooking liquid into a saucepan. Add the cornflour paste and heat gently, stirring constantly, until thickened. Reduce the heat and simmer for at least 5 minutes. Remove from the heat. Add the mustard and season to taste with pepper.

4 Place the fish, egg quarters and vegetables in an ovenproof dish. Pour over the sauce. Top with the mashed potatoes. Bake in a preheated oven, 180°C (350°F), Gas Mark 4, for 20 minutes.

5 Garnish with tomatoes and return to the oven for 5 minutes. Serve with peas or baked beans, if liked.

500 g (1 lb) white fish, such as a
mixture of smoked and
unsmoked cod or haddock
300 ml (½ pint) skimmed milk
1 bay leaf
1 teaspoon olive oil
1 onion, finely chopped
1 carrot, finely chopped
2 large handfuls of spinach
leaves
1 tablespoon cornflour, blended
with a little cold water
1 teaspoon mustard
2 hard-boiled eggs, shelled and
quartered
500 g (1 lb) cooked potatoes,
mashed with semi-skimmed
milk and unsaturated spread
freshly ground black pepper
sliced tomatoes, to garnish

potato & olive bread

Preparation time: 25 minutes, plus proving
Cooking time: 40 minutes

(V)

Makes 1 loaf

NUTRITIONAL FACTS* ● kcals – 1840 (7801 kJ) ● Fat – 23 g, of which 5 g saturated ● Sodium – 1220 mg

1 Place the mashed potatoes in a large bowl with the flour. Blend the fresh yeast with the milk. If using dried yeast, dissolve the sugar in the milk, then sprinkle over the yeast and leave in a warm place for about 10 minutes until frothy. Add the yeast mixture and water to the dry ingredients and mix to form a fairly firm dough.

2 Turn on to a floured surface and knead for about 10 minutes until smooth and even. Shape into a ball, place inside an oiled plastic bag and leave in a warm place until doubled in size.

3 Turn out the dough and knead until smooth, adding two-thirds of the olives. Make into a loaf-like shape or shape to fit a greased 1 kg (2 lb) loaf tin. Cover with the oiled plastic bag and leave to prove in a warm place until the dough reaches the top of the tin. Remove the plastic bag and sprinkle with the remaining olives.

4 Bake in a preheated oven, 220°C (425°F), Gas Mark 7, for about 40 minutes, either on a baking sheet if cooking it free-form or in the loaf tin, until the base of the loaf sounds hollow when tapped. Cool on a wire rack.

*figures for whole loaf

125 g (4 oz) cooked potatoes, mashed with 1 tablespoon unsaturated spread
500 g (1 lb) strong white plain flour
15 g (½ oz) fresh yeast or 1½ level teaspoons dried yeast plus 1 teaspoon sugar
150 ml (¼ pint) warm milk
150 ml (¼ pint) warm water
15 pitted black olives, thinly sliced

NUTRITIONAL TIPS

Bread can contain a surprising amount of salt, so by making your own you can limit the amount. This unusual bread contains a reasonable amount of salt because there are 70 mg sodium in each black olive. Rinse the olives and dry them thoroughly on kitchen paper before slicing them, to remove some of the salt.

garlic mash

Preparation time: 10 minutes   (V)   **Serves 4**
Cooking time: 1¼ hours
NUTRITIONAL FACTS   ❍ kcals – 185 (777 kJ)   ❍ Fat – less than 1 g, of which a trace saturated   ❍ Sodium – 24 mg

1 Prick the potatoes with a fork and bake in a preheated oven, 220°C (425°F), Gas Mark 7, for 1¼ hours until tender.

2 Meanwhile, remove the outer skin from the head of garlic but do not separate the cloves. Slice off the top. Wrap in foil, shiny side inwards. Place on a baking sheet and roast on a lower shelf in the oven for 45 minutes until the garlic flesh is softened to a purée.

3 Holding the baked potato with an oven glove, pierce a cross in the top of each potato with a fork. Squeeze so that the flesh rises up through the skin. Scoop into a bowl and mash with a fork. (Save the crunchy skins for a snack.) Squeeze the roasted garlic flesh into the potatoes and mash thoroughly. Mix in the stock and milk, a tablespoon of each at a time, until the desired texture is achieved. Season to taste with pepper, then stir in the chives (if using).

1 firm head of garlic
3 baking potatoes, about 300 g (10 oz) each, scrubbed
3–4 tablespoons warm Vegetable Stock (see page 122)
3–4 tablespoons warm skimmed milk
1 tablespoon snipped chives (optional)
freshly ground black pepper

OR YOU COULD TRY...
CHEESE MASH: Replace the stock and milk with 1–2 tablespoons natural fromage frais or yogurt and 2–3 tablespoons Parmesan cheese.
CELERIAC MASH: Mash potatoes with 375 g (12 oz) peeled, chopped and boiled celeriac. Add skimmed milk, a little unsaturated spread and nutmeg.

NUTRITIONAL TIPS
Baked potatoes make the best mashed potatoes – smooth, rich and creamy – and if you follow this recipe they are surprisingly low in fat. The warm roasted garlic is also ideal for spreading straight on to French bread.

simply baked potatoes

Preparation time: 5 minutes
Cooking time: 75 minutes

Serves 4
N U T R I T I O N A L   F A C T S * ❍ kcals – 400 (1680 kJ) ❍ Fat – less than 1 g, of which negligible saturated ❍ Sodium – 36 mg

1 Bake the potatoes directly on the shelf in a preheated oven, 220°C (425°F), Gas Mark 7, for 1¼ hours until tender. You can shorten the cooking time by using potato bakers, pots or even skewers, or by halving very large potatoes.

2 Cut a cross in the top of each potato and spoon in your choice of filling to serve. Or cut the top off each potato and carefully scoop out most of the flesh. Mash with your choice of filling and pile back in the skins. Serve or stand on a baking sheet and return to the oven or place under a moderate grill for 5 minutes until reheated and beginning to brown.

OR YOU COULD TRY...

CURRIED PRAWN AND COURGETTE TOPPING
Place 1 finely chopped onion with a little water in a saucepan over a low heat and cook for about 5 minutes until soft. Stir in 1 teaspoon of turmeric, 2 tablespoons mild curry paste, 1 grated courgette, 250 g (8 oz) prawns and a little more water if necessary. Heat through gently. Use to top the baked potatoes when cooked. A serving of this topping would provide you with 100 kcals (420 kJ), 2 g of fat or which less than 1 g is saturated and 1109 mg of sodium in addition to the nutritional facts for each baked potato.

* figures for each 300g (10 oz) baked potato

4 baking potatoes in their skins, each 250–375 g (8–12 oz)
a little vegetable oil (optional)
freshly ground black pepper

OR YOU COULD TRY...
More fillings and toppings:
❍ Thai Beef and Pepper Stir-fry (see page 100)
❍ Smoked salmon and chopped chives
❍ Crispy lean bacon, apricots and celery
❍ Grated low-fat cheese with chopped shallots
❍ Flaked tuna, sweetcorn and natural fromage frais
❍ Prawns with spring onions and natural yogurt
❍ Cottage cheese with pineapple

N U T R I T I O N A L   T I P S
Baked potatoes have great nutritional value. They are a good source of both vitamin C and fibre, which is in their 'jackets', so make sure you eat the crispy skin.

tagliatelle with bacon, mushrooms & pine nuts

Preparation time: 10 minutes   **Serves 4**
Cooking time: 10 minutes
NUTRITIONAL FACTS   ○ kcals – 535 (2247 kJ)   ○ Fat – 14 g, of which 2 g saturated   ○ Sodium – 740 mg

1 Cook the tagliatelle according to the packet instructions.

2 Meanwhile, heat the oil in a nonstick frying pan, add the pepper and cook for 2–3 minutes. Stir in the garlic, mushrooms, bacon, parsley and pepper to taste.

3 Reduce the heat and stir in the fromage frais or yogurt. Heat through very gently.

4 Drain the pasta and toss with the sauce. Sprinkle with the pine nuts before serving. Serve with an Italian-style salad and fresh ciabatta bread.

375 g (12 oz) green and white
   tagliatelle
1 tablespoon olive oil
1 yellow pepper, cored, deseeded
   and chopped
2 teaspoons garlic purée, or
   crushed garlic
125 g (4 oz) button mushrooms,
   sliced
125 g (4 oz) rindless lean back
   bacon, grilled and cut into
   thin strips
1 tablespoon chopped parsley
500 g (1 lb) natural fromage frais
   or yogurt
25 g (1 oz) pine nuts, toasted
freshly ground black pepper

lean lasagne

Preparation time: 30 minutes **Serves 8**
Cooking time: about 1 hour
NUTRITIONAL FACTS   ○ kcals – 340 (1428 kJ)   ○ Fat – 11 g, of which 5 g saturated   ○ Sodium – 180 mg

1 For the meat sauce, place the aubergines, onions, garlic, stock and wine in a large nonstick saucepan. Cover and simmer briskly for 5 minutes.

2 Uncover and cook for about 5 minutes until the aubergine is tender and the liquid is absorbed, adding a little more stock if necessary. Remove from the heat, allow to cool slightly, then purée in a food processor or blender.

3 Meanwhile, brown the mince in a nonstick frying pan. Drain off any fat. Add the aubergine mixture, tomatoes and pepper to taste. Simmer briskly, uncovered, for about 10 minutes until thickened.

4 For the cheese sauce, beat the egg whites with the ricotta. Beat in the milk and 4 tablespoons of Parmesan. Season to taste with pepper.

5 To make the lasagne, alternate layers of meat sauce, lasagne and cheese sauce. Start with meat sauce and finish with cheese sauce. Sprinkle with the remaining Parmesan. Bake in a preheated oven, 180°C (350°F), Gas Mark 4, for 30–40 minutes until browned.

200 g (7 oz) pre-cooked sheets
  of lasagne
freshly ground black pepper

MEAT SAUCE
2 aubergines, peeled and diced
2 red onions, chopped
2 garlic cloves, crushed
300 ml (½ pint) Vegetable Stock
  (see page 122)
4 tablespoons red wine
500 g (1 lb) extra-lean mince
2 x 400 g (13 oz) cans chopped
  tomatoes

CHEESE SAUCE
3 egg whites
250 g (8 oz) ricotta cheese
175 ml (6 fl oz) skimmed milk
6 tablespoons freshly grated
  Parmesan cheese

NUTRITIONAL TIPS
Despite its Mediterranean origins, lasagne can be even higher in fat and calories than fried foods. In this reduced-fat version, the white sauce is made from low-fat ricotta cheese, which tastes sweet and creamy.

macaroni cheese surprise

Preparation time: 15 minutes   (V)   **Serves 4**

Cooking time: 40 minutes

NUTRITIONAL FACTS   O kcals – 308 (1293 kJ)   O Fat – 6 g, of which 3 g saturated   O Sodium – 255 mg

1 Cook the macaroni according to the packet instructions until just tender and drain.

2 Meanwhile, lightly cook all the vegetables so that they remain crunchy. Drain well.

3 Mix the cornflour and a little of the milk together in a saucepan. Blend to a smooth paste. Heat gently, adding the rest of the milk and whisking continuously until the sauce boils and thickens. Add three-quarters of the cheese, the mustard and cayenne pepper to taste.

4 Mix together the pasta, vegetables and sauce and spoon into an ovenproof dish. Scatter with the remaining cheese and sprinkle with a little cayenne pepper to garnish. Bake in a preheated oven, 200°C (400°F), Gas Mark 6, for about 25 minutes, until golden brown.

OR YOU COULD TRY...

Any vegetables, lightly cooked and added to the cheesy mixture, such as peas, sweetcorn, mixed peppers, mushrooms and mixed vegetables.

175 g (6 oz) wholemeal macaroni
2 carrots, cut into small, chunky batons
250 g (8 oz) broccoli florets
1 large leek, trimmed and thickly sliced
50 g (2 oz) cornflour
600 ml (1 pint) skimmed milk
100 g (3½ oz) low-fat mature hard cheese, grated
1 teaspoon mustard
pinch of cayenne pepper, plus extra to garnish

NUTRITIONAL TIPS
All pasta is naturally healthy – rich in carbohydrates and low in fat. Wholemeal pasta is made from the whole grain and contains more insoluble fibre than the white variety. This type of fibre helps to prevent constipation and other bowel problems.

farfalle with anchovy & oregano sauce

Preparation time: 10 minutes   **Serves 4**

Cooking time: 15 minutes

NUTRITIONAL FACTS   ● kcals – 390 (1653 kJ)   ● Fat – 7 g, of which less than 1 g saturated   ● Sodium – 500 mg

1 Heat the oil in a small saucepan, add the garlic and fry gently for about 5 minutes until golden.

2 Reduce the heat to very low, stir in the anchovies and cook very gently for about 10 minutes until they have completely disintegrated.

3 Meanwhile, cook the pasta according to the packet instructions until just tender.

4 Stir the oregano and pepper to taste into the sauce.

5 Drain the pasta and turn into a warmed serving dish. Pour over the sauce, sprinkle with the parsley and gently toss together. Serve with Parmesan cheese and a crisp Mediterranean salad, if liked.

1 tablespoon olive oil

2 garlic cloves, finely chopped

50 g (2 oz) canned anchovy fillets, drained

375 g (12 oz) dried farfalle

2 teaspoons oregano, finely chopped

3 tablespoons chopped parsley

freshly ground black pepper

grated Parmesan cheese, to serve

NUTRITIONAL TIPS

All pasta has a very low glycaemic index (GI). This is because it is made from high-protein semolina (finely cracked wheat) and has a dense food matrix that resists disruption in the small intestine. But even pasta made from fine flour instead of semolina has a relatively low GI. Interestingly, there is some evidence that thicker pasta has a lower GI than thin varieties.

wild rice jambalaya

Preparation time: 15 minutes

Serves 4

Cooking time: 35 minutes

NUTRITIONAL FACTS   ◯ kcals – 370 (1554 kJ)   ◯ Fat – 3 g, of which less than 1 g saturated   ◯ Sodium – 680 mg

1 Place the wild rice in a saucepan with water to cover. Bring to the boil and boil for 5 minutes. Remove the pan from the heat and cover tightly. Leave to steam for about 10 minutes until the grains are tender. Drain.

2 Heat the oil in a large nonstick frying pan. Add the celery, peppers, onion, bacon and garlic. Cook, stirring, for 3–4 minutes until the vegetables are soft. Stir in the tomato purée and thyme. Cook for another 2 minutes.

3 Add the wild rice, long-grain rice, chilli, cayenne pepper, pimientos (if using), tomatoes, stock and wine. Bring to the boil. Reduce the heat and simmer for 10 minutes until the rice is tender but still firm to the bite.

4 Add the prawns or mycoprotein and cook, stirring occasionally, for 5 minutes, until the prawns have turned opaque. Spoon into large warmed bowls. Scatter with coriander or parsley and serve. Accompany with crusty bread, if liked.

125 g (4 oz) wild rice
1 teaspoon olive oil
50 g (2 oz) celery, chopped
½ red pepper, cored, deseeded and diced
½ green or yellow pepper, cored, deseeded and diced
1 onion, chopped
1 rindless lean back bacon rasher, trimmed of fat
2 garlic cloves, crushed
2 tablespoons tomato purée
1 tablespoon chopped thyme
125 g (4 oz) long-grain rice
1 green chilli, deseeded and finely chopped
½ teaspoon cayenne pepper
1 tablespoon chopped canned pimientos (optional)
400 g (13 oz) can tomatoes, drained
300 ml (½ pint) Chicken Stock (see page 122)
150 ml (¼ pint) dry white wine
250 g (8 oz) raw medium prawns or mycoprotein pieces
3 tablespoons chopped fresh coriander or parsley, to garnish

chicken, wild mushroom & fennel rice

Preparation time: 10 minutes   **Serves 4**
Cooking time: 30 minutes

N U T R I T I O N A L   F A C T S   ○ kcals – 440 (1848 kJ)   ○ Fat – 10 g, of which 1 g saturated   ○ Sodium – 260 mg

1 Heat the oil in a saucepan and gently fry the fennel, onion and garlic for 5 minutes. Add the mushrooms and cook for 2 minutes. Stir in the rice and gently fry for 2 minutes. Add the wine and stir until absorbed by the rice.

2 Add half the stock and bring to the boil, then lower the heat and simmer gently, stirring frequently, until absorbed. Add the rest of the stock a little at a time, allowing each amount to be absorbed before adding the next.

3 After about 15 minutes, add the chicken, dill and lemon rind and juice. Cook for about 5 minutes more, until the rice is creamy but still firm to the bite. Season to taste with pepper and turn into a warmed serving dish. Sprinkle with pine nuts and garnish with dill sprigs.

1 tablespoon olive oil
1 fennel bulb, trimmed and
    finely sliced
1 onion, finely sliced
1 garlic clove, crushed
175 g (6 oz) mixed mushrooms,
    including some wild, sliced
250 g (8 oz) basmati rice
150 ml ($\frac{1}{4}$ pint) dry white wine
450 ml ($\frac{3}{4}$ pint) Chicken Stock
    (see page 122)
250 g (8 oz) cooked chicken,
    diced
$\frac{1}{2}$ bunch of dill, finely chopped,
finely grated rind and juice of
    1 lemon
freshly ground black pepper
25 g (1 oz) pine nuts, toasted
dill sprigs, to garnish

N U T R I T I O N A L   T I P S
Traditional Asian-style diets, characterized by relatively large quantities of rice and small quantities of meat, offer many heart-health benefits. Paella mirrors this principle and can be made with a variety of ingredients such as vegetables, fish and meat.

red kidney bean & aubergine pilaf

Preparation time: 15 minutes   (V)   **Serves 4**
Cooking time: 40 minutes
N U T R I T I O N A L   F A C T S   ○ kcals – 330 (1386 kJ)   ○ Fat – 7 g, of which 1 g saturated   ○ Sodium – 144 mg

1 Place the water in a large saucepan and bring to the boil. Add the rice and turmeric and stir well to prevent the rice from sticking. Cover and simmer for 30 minutes without stirring. Remove from the heat.

2 Meanwhile, heat the oil in a nonstick frying pan, add the onion, garlic, celery, pepper and aubergine and cook gently for 3 minutes without browning. Add the tomatoes and mushrooms, stir well and cook for 3–4 minutes.

3 Stir the beans and the vegetable mixture into the rice, cover and cook very gently for 10 minutes.

4 Remove from the heat and leave for 5 minutes. Season to taste with pepper and stir in the parsley. Transfer to a warmed serving dish to serve.

OR YOU COULD TRY...
Adding two 275 g (9 oz) cooked and chopped boneless, skinless chicken joints before the tomatoes and mushrooms, for an alternative non-vegetarian supper.

450 ml (¾ pint) water
250 g (8 oz) brown long-grain rice
½ teaspoon turmeric
1 tablespoon vegetable oil
1 large onion, finely chopped
1 garlic clove, finely chopped
1 celery stick, chopped
1 green pepper, cored, deseeded and chopped
1 aubergine, diced
2 tomatoes, skinned and chopped
125 g (4 oz) mushrooms, sliced
200 g (7 oz) canned kidney beans, rinsed and drained
2 tablespoons chopped parsley
freshly ground black pepper

N U T R I T I O N A L   T I P S
Beans are a good source of protein, especially when they are served with a cereal food such as rice, bread or pasta. They are low in fat, high in fibre and rich in many nutrients, providing iron, zinc, calcium, folate and soluble fibre.

tomato & herb pizza pie

Preparation time: 15 minutes   (V)   **Serves 6**
Cooking time: 35–40 minutes

NUTRITIONAL FACTS   O kcals – 340 (1428 kJ)   O Fat – 15g, of which 5 g saturated   O Sodium – 268 mg

1 For the scone base, sieve the flour into a mixing bowl and rub in the spread until the mixture resembles fine breadcrumbs. Add just enough milk to form a soft dough. Turn out on to a lightly floured surface and knead until smooth. Roll out to a 23–25 cm (9–10 inches) diameter round, then place on a greased baking sheet.

2 For the topping, heat the oil in a large saucepan, add the onion and garlic and fry gently for 5 minutes until softened. Add the pepper, tomatoes, tomato purée and basil or thyme and simmer, uncovered, for about 10 minutes until the mixture is thick. Season with pepper.

3 Spread the tomato mixture over the base to the edge. Top with the cheese. Bake in the centre of a preheated oven, 220°C (425°F), Gas Mark 7, for 20–25 minutes until the topping is bubbling. Garnish with basil sprigs before serving.

OR YOU COULD TRY...

- o Anchovy fillets and black olives
- o Red onion, feta cheese, red pepper and rocket
- o Spinach and ricotta
- o Caponata Ratatouille (see page 48)

BASE
300 g (10 oz) wholemeal self-raising flour
50 g (2 oz) unsaturated spread
150 ml (¼ pint) skimmed milk

TOPPING
1 tablespoon olive oil
2 large onions, chopped
1–2 garlic cloves
1 green or red pepper, cored, deseeded and sliced
2 x 400 g (13 oz) cans tomatoes
2 tablespoons tomato purée
large handful of basil or thyme, chopped
125 g (4 oz) low-fat mozzarella cheese, sliced
freshly ground black pepper
basil sprigs, to garnish

NUTRITIONAL TIPS
Home-made pizzas can be very healthy, with a starchy base topped with your own choice of fresh vegetables and low-fat ingredients. Look out for half-fat mozzarella, which has only 10 g of fat per 100 g (3½ oz).

thai sesame & tofu stir-fry

Preparation time: 15 minutes   **V**   **Serves 4**
Cooking time: 10 minutes
NUTRITIONAL FACTS   ○ kcals – 400 (1680 kJ)   ○ Fat – 12 g, of which 2 g saturated   ○ Sodium – 400 mg

1 In a small bowl, mix together the sesame oil and 1 tablespoon Teriyaki Sauce. Brush the mixture over both sides of the tofu. Sprinkle one side of each piece of tofu with half the sesame seeds. Mix together the remaining Teriyaki Sauce, vinegar and soy sauce. Set aside.

2 Heat a large wok or frying pan. Brush with a little of the groundnut oil. Add the tofu, seed side down, and cook for 2 minutes. Sprinkle the remaining sesame seeds over the tofu. Turn over and cook for 2 minutes more until crisp. Remove the tofu from the pan and keep warm.

3 Brush the pan with a little more groundnut oil, then add the mangetouts, carrot, bean sprouts and spring onion batons. Stir-fry for 2–3 minutes until tender yet still crisp. Add the reserved teriyaki sauce mixture. Stir-fry for 1 minute.

4 Divide the hot noodles between warmed serving bowls. Add the watercress, spoon over the vegetables and top with the tofu. Garnish with the shredded spring onion. Serve with a green salad, if liked.

1 teaspoon sesame oil
2 tablespoons Teriyaki Sauce (see page 124)
400 g (13 oz) firm tofu, cut into 4 thick slices
2 tablespoons sesame seeds
1 tablespoon rice wine vinegar
2 teaspoons low-salt soy sauce
1 tablespoon groundnut oil
16 mangetouts
1 carrot, cut into thin strips
125 g (4 oz) bean sprouts
2 spring onions, white parts cut into 5 cm (2 inch) batons, green tops shredded for garnish
250 g (8 oz) rice noodles, prepared as packet instructions
50 g (2 oz) watercress sprigs

NUTRITIONAL TIPS
Tofu (soya bean curd) is rich in protein and B vitamins, low in saturated fat and sodium and an important non-dairy source of calcium.

vegetarian cider & sage sausages

Preparation time: 10 minutes

Cooking time: 35–45 minutes

Serves 4

NUTRITIONAL FACTS   ❍ kcals – 200 (840 kJ)   ❍ Fat – 3.5 g, of which 2 g saturated   ❍ Sodium – 200 mg

1 Heat a flameproof casserole. Add the sausages and cook for 8–10 minutes, turning frequently, until browned all over. Remove and set aside.

2 Pour a little water into the pan, add the vegetables and simmer gently for about 5 minutes, stirring, until lightly coloured. Stir in the flour and cook for 1–2 minutes.

3 Pour in the cider and stock and bring to the boil, stirring. Reduce the heat and return the sausages to the pan. Season to taste with pepper and add the sage. Cover and cook for 20–30 minutes, stirring occasionally, adding a little more stock if necessary. Serve with Garlic Mash (see page 72), if liked.

6 vegetarian or mycoprotein (Quorn) sausages
1 onion, sliced
2 celery sticks, sliced
2 carrots, sliced
1 green pepper, cored, deseeded and sliced
2 tablespoons plain flour
300 ml (½ pint) medium-dry cider
150 ml–300 ml (¼–½ pint) homemade Vegetable Stock (see page 122)
1 teaspoon dried sage
freshly ground black pepper

easy bean & pepper bake

Preparation time: 10 minutes   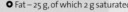   **Serves 4**

Cooking time: 30–40 minutes

NUTRITIONAL FACTS   O Kcals – 384 (1613 kJ)   O Fat – 25 g, of which 2 g saturated   O Sodium – 586 mg

1 In a large bowl, mix together all the beans, blended tomatoes or passata, onion, herbs, garlic, fennel or celery, peppers and pepper to taste.

2 Brush an ovenproof dish with a little oil. Pour in the bean mixture and top with the chopped tomatoes.

3 Bake in a preheated oven, 180°C (350°F), Gas Mark 4, for 35–40 minutes. Serve sprinkled with Parmesan. Accompany with wild rice, broccoli and steamed carrots and parsnips, if liked.

325 g (11 oz) can borlotti beans, rinsed and drained

400 g (13 oz) can butter beans, rinsed and drained

400 g (13 oz) can flageolet beans, rinsed and drained

400 g (13 oz) blended tomatoes or passata

1 large onion, chopped

2 teaspoons dried Italian herbs

2 teaspoons chopped parsley

1 garlic clove, finely chopped

1 bulb of fennel, or celery, sliced

2 red or green pepper, cored, deseeded and chopped

a little vegetable oil, for brushing

2 tomatoes, chopped

freshly ground black pepper

3 tablespoons grated Parmesan cheese, to serve

NUTRITIONAL TIPS

Beans are high in soluble and insoluble fibre. Soluble fibre helps lower blood cholesterol and control blood sugar levels, while insoluble fibre helps to prevent bowel problems.

mixed masala beans

Preparation time: 5 minutes (V) **Serves 4**
Cooking time: 30 minutes
NUTRITIONAL FACTS ● kcals – 150 (630 kJ) ● Fat – 5 g, of which 0.5 g saturated ● Sodium – 315 mg

1 Heat the oil in a heavy-based saucepan, add the onion and cumin seeds and fry gently for about 5 minutes until lightly golden. Stir in the other spices. Add the 2 tablespoons water and cook, stirring continuously, for 1–2 minutes.

2 Gently stir in the chickpeas, kidney beans, tomato, chillies, garlic and ginger. Mix well and stir in the 250 ml (8 fl oz) water. Bring to the boil, then reduce the heat and simmer for 15–20 minutes.

3 Add the pepper and cook for another 2–3 minutes. Stir in the lemon juice and half the coriander. Serve immediately, garnished with the remaining coriander.

OR YOU COULD TRY...
Serving this versatile dish with basmati rice and a crisp green salad, as a vegetable side dish with Tandoori Chicken (see page 104) or Kofta Curry (see page 106) as a topping for baked potatoes (see page 73) or cold as a salad.

1 tablespoon vegetable oil
1 small onion, chopped
½ teaspoon cumin seeds
½ teaspoon chilli powder
½ teaspoon turmeric
¼ teaspoon garam masala
250 ml (8 fl oz) water, plus
   2 tablespoons
200 g (7 oz) can chickpeas,
   rinsed and drained
200 g (7 oz) can red kidney
   beans, rinsed and drained
1 tomato, chopped
1–2 green chillies, deseeded and
   chopped
4 garlic cloves, finely chopped
1 teaspoon finely grated fresh
   root ginger
1 green pepper, cored, deseeded
   and chopped
2 teaspoons lemon juice
2–3 tablespoons fresh coriander
   leaves, chopped

NUTRITIONAL TIPS
Beans are an excellent source of phytoestrogens which possess antiviral, antibacterial, anticarcinogenic and antifungal properties.

chilli bean & corn stuffed peppers

Preparation time: 15 minutes

Cooking time: about 1 hour

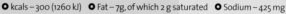

Serves 4

NUTRITIONAL FACTS ❍ kcals – 300 (1260 kJ) ❍ Fat – 7g, of which 2 g saturated ❍ Sodium – 425 mg

1 Place the rice in a large saucepan of cold water and bring to the boil. Reduce the heat and simmer for 20–25 minutes until tender. Drain and place in a bowl.

2 Meanwhile, place the oil in a saucepan, add the onion and fry gently for 5 minutes. Add this to the rice with the chilli powder, sweetcorn and beans. Season to taste with pepper.

3 Slice the tops off the peppers and reserve. Shave a little off the bottoms so that they sit upright, then remove and discard the cores and seeds. Stand on a baking sheet.

4 Stir the cheese into the rice mixture and pile into the peppers, packing down well. Replace the pepper tops. Bake in a preheated oven, 200°C (400°F), Gas Mark 6, for 30 minutes until tender. Serve with natural yogurt, if liked.

75 g (3 oz) easy-cook brown rice
1 tablespoon vegetable oil
1 onion, finely chopped
½ teaspoon hot chilli powder
200 g (7 oz) canned sweetcorn, rinsed and drained
200 g (7 oz) canned kidney beans, rinsed and drained
4 red peppers
50 g (2 oz) low-fat mature hard cheese, grated
freshly ground black pepper
natural yogurt, to serve

OR YOU COULD TRY...
Using this filling to stuff the following vegetables: aubergines, onions, mushrooms, potatoes, gem squash, butternut squash, tomatoes, savoy cabbage leaves, vine leaves, courgettes and marrows.

NUTRITIONAL TIPS
Highly convenient to use, canned pulses, baked beans, sweetcorn and peas, are essential items for your healthy-heart storecupboard. By adding beans to any of your dishes, you can help reduce your risk of heart disease.

tomato & mushroom soya bolognese

Preparation time: 15 minutes   **Serves 4**

Cooking time: 20–25 minutes

N U T R I T I O N A L   F A C T S   ○ Kcals – 195 (819 kJ)   ○ Fat – 5 g, of which 0.5g saturated   ○ Sodium – 2011 mg

1 Prepare the soya mince according to the packet instructions.

2 Heat the oil in a large saucepan, add the onion and garlic and cook, stirring, for 2–3 minutes until softened.

3 Add the mushrooms, carrot, tomatoes, stock, tomato purée, herbs, yeast extract, soya mince and pepper to taste. Stir well, then simmer for 20–25 minutes.

4 Meanwhile, cook the spaghetti according to the packet instructions until just tender. Drain well.

5 Serve the spaghetti topped with the sauce and sprinkled with a little Parmesan. Accompany with a green leafy salad, if liked.

150 g (5 oz) dried soya mince
1 tablespoon vegetable oil
1 onion, chopped
1 garlic clove, crushed
125 g (4 oz) mushrooms, sliced
1 carrot, sliced
1 kg (2 lb) ripe tomatoes,
 skinned, or 2 x 400 g (13 oz)
 cans chopped tomatoes
150 ml (¼ pint) Vegetable Stock
 (see page 122)
2 tablespoons tomato purée
1 teaspoon dried oregano
1 teaspoon dried basil
1 teaspoon yeast extract
400 g (13 oz) dried spaghetti
freshly ground black pepper
grated Parmesan cheese, to
 serve

cashew & green pepper risotto

Preparation time: 5 minutes   **Serves 5**
Cooking time: 55 minutes
NUTRITIONAL FACTS   ● kcals – 421 (1768 kJ)   ● Fat – 16 g, of which 3 g saturated   ● Sodium – 410 mg

1 Heat the oil in a large frying pan or wok, add the onion and pepper and fry gently for about 5 minutes until softened. Add the sweetcorn and rice and cook, stirring, for 1 minute.

2 Stir in the stock and bring to the boil. Reduce the heat and simmer, uncovered, for 30–40 minutes until the rice is tender.

3 Stir in the soy sauce and cashew nuts and cook for a further 5–10 minutes until all the stock is absorbed. Serve with a mixed salad, if liked, or as a side dish.

2 teaspoons vegetable oil
1 onion, finely sliced
1 green pepper, cored, deseeded and finely sliced
125 g (4 oz) sweetcorn
300 g (10 oz) brown rice
900 ml (1½ pints) hot Vegetable Stock (see page 122)
1 tablespoon reduced-salt soy sauce
125 g (4 oz) unsalted cashew nuts

NUTRITIONAL TIPS
Research suggests that eating a small handful of unsalted nuts (25 g/1 oz) on most days can lower cholesterol and reduce the risk of a heart attack. Although high in fat, nuts make a healthy substitute for snacks like crisps and biscuits.

lentil & vegetable khichiri

Preparation time: 10 minutes, plus soaking
Cooking time: 35 minutes

Serves 4

NUTRITIONAL FACTS   ● Kcals – 300 (1260 kJ)   ● Fat – 8 g, of which 1 g saturated   ● Sodium – 26 mg

1 Wash the lentils and rice together, then soak in a bowl of water for 15–20 minutes. Drain and set aside.

2 Heat the oil in a saucepan, add the onion, cinnamon, cardamom (if using), cumin seeds and cloves and fry gently for about 5 minutes, stirring frequently, until the onion turns a deep golden colour.

3 Add the turmeric, chilli powder, ginger and garlic paste, yogurt and a little water and cook for 2–3 minutes, adding a little more water if necessary. Stir in the beans, carrot and tomato and cook for 1–2 minutes.

4 Add the rice and lentils, stir to mix, then add the measured water. Cover the pan with a close-fitting lid and bring to the boil. Reduce the heat and simmer for 20 minutes, then allow to stand for 3–4 minutes before serving.

50 g (2 oz) red lentils
200 g (7 oz) basmati or
   long-grain rice
2 tablespoons vegetable oil
1 onion, finely chopped
1 cm (½ inch) piece of cinnamon
   stick
1 black cardamom pod, split or
   bruised (optional)
1 teaspoon cumin seeds
2–3 cloves
¼ teaspoon turmeric
½ teaspoon chilli powder
2 teaspoons Ginger and Garlic
   Paste (see page 123)
1 tablespoon natural yogurt
75 g (3 oz) green beans, chopped
75 g (3 oz) carrot, diced
50 g (2 oz) tomato, chopped
450 ml (¾ pint) water

NUTRITIONAL TIPS
Pulses including lentils, chickpeas, soya beans and kidney beans are an important part of a low glycaemic index (GI) diet. It is recommended that you try to eat beans – either dried or canned – at least twice a week.

aubergine & potato soya moussaka

1 Heat most of the oil in a nonstick frying pan and fry the aubergines in batches for about 10 minutes until lightly browned. Set aside. Repeat with the potato slices, carefully adding a little boiling water or stock if necessary. Set aside with the aubergine.

2 Add the onion to the pan and cook for 5 minutes. Add the soya mince and cook for 5 minutes. Add the wine, stock, passata, tomato purée, spices, thyme and pepper to taste. Gently simmer, uncovered, for about 15 minutes until thickened. Remove from the heat.

3 For the topping, blend the cornflour with a little of the milk. Place in a saucepan over a low heat and gradually whisk in the remaining milk. Continue stirring until the sauce thickens. Simmer for 2–3 minutes. Stir in the nutmeg and allow to cool before whisking in the egg.

4 Brush an ovenproof dish with the remaining oil. Place a layer of potato in the bottom, cover with a layer of the sauce, followed by a layer of aubergines. Continue layering in this order. Pour the topping over the dish and sprinkle with Parmesan. Bake in a preheated oven, 190°C (375°F), Gas Mark 5, for about 45 minutes until browned.

1 tablespoon olive oil

2 medium aubergines, thinly sliced

2 large potatoes, thinly sliced

1 large onion, chopped

150 g (5 oz) dried soya mince, prepared according to packet instructions

300 ml (½ pint) red wine

300 ml (½ pint) Vegetable Stock (see page 122)

300 ml (½ pint) passata

2 tablespoons tomato purée

½ teaspoon ground cinnamon

¼ teaspoon ground nutmeg

½ teaspoon dried thyme

freshly ground black pepper

25 g (1 oz) cornflour

450 ml (¾ pint) skimmed milk

¼ teaspoon ground nutmeg

1 egg

50 g (2 oz) Parmesan cheese, grated

> **NUTRITIONAL TIPS**
> *To reduce the amount of oil used in frying vegetables, add a little hot stock or wine or sherry so that they sauté or steam in their own juices.*

sweet potato & cannellini falafel

Preparation time: 20 minutes   (V)   **Serves 6**
Cooking time: 10 minutes
NUTRITIONAL FACTS   ● kcals – 215 (903 kJ)   ● Fat – 8 g, of which 1 g saturated   ● Sodium – 245 mg

1 Boil or microwave the sweet potato until tender, then drain. Place in a bowl and mash. Set aside.

2 Heat the oil in a nonstick frying pan, add the garlic, cumin and ground coriander. Cook, stirring, for 1–2 minutes until fragrant. Stir in the tomato purée. Cook for 3–4 minutes until the mixture becomes deep red and develops a rich aroma. Stir in the beans.

3 Place the fresh coriander, tahini and lemon juice in a food processor or blender and process to form a coarse paste.

4 Mix the bean mixture and breadcrumbs with the sweet potato. Shape the mixture into 2.5 cm (1 inch) round patties. If the mixture feels too wet to shape into patties you may need to add some extra breadcrumbs. Roll in flour to coat. Place on a plate lined with clingfilm. Cover and refrigerate until ready to cook – the patties can be made up to 1 day in advance.

5 Grill the falafel under a preheated hot grill for 3–4 minutes each side until golden and crispy.

6 Spread the bread with hummus. Top with lettuce, tabbouleh and onion. Place 3 falafel in each pitta and flatten slightly. Sprinkle with lemon juice to taste and serve immediately.

6 pitta breads, warmed
1 tablespoon low-fat hummus or Tahini Hummus (see page 29)
100 g (3½ oz) shredded lettuce
175 g Tabbouleh (see page 44)
1 red onion, thinly sliced
lemon juice, to serve

FALAFEL
400 g (13 oz) orange sweet potato, cut into chunks
2 teaspoons olive oil
1 clove garlic, crushed
2 teaspoons ground cumin
1 teaspoon ground coriander
1 tablespoon tomato purée
400 g (13 oz) can cannellini beans, rinsed and drained
2 tablespoons chopped fresh coriander leaves
1 tablespoon tahini (sesame seed paste)
1 tablespoon lemon juice
75 g (3 oz) dry breadcrumbs
flour, for coating

thai beef & mixed pepper stir-fry

Preparation time: 20 minutes   **Serves 4**
Cooking time: 10 minutes
NUTRITIONAL FACTS* ◑ kcals – 255 (1067 kJ) ◑ Fat – 12 g, of which 3 g saturated ◑ Sodium – 4 mg

1 Cut the beef into long, thin strips, cutting across the grain.

2 Heat the oil in a wok or large frying pan over a high heat. Add the garlic and stir-fry for 1 minute.

3 Add the beef and stir-fry for 2–3 minutes until lightly coloured. Stir in the lemon grass and ginger and remove the pan from the heat. Remove the beef from the pan and set side.

4 Add the peppers and onion and stir-fry for 2–3 minutes until the onions are just turning golden brown and are slightly softened.

5 Return the beef to the pan, stir in the lime juice and season to taste with pepper. Serve with boiled noodles or rice, if liked.

*figures per serving without noodles or rice

500 g (1 lb) lean beef fillet
1 tablespoon sesame oil
1 garlic clove, finely chopped
1 lemon grass stalk, finely
  shredded
2.5 cm (1 inch) piece of fresh root
  ginger, peeled and finely
  chopped
1 red pepper, cored, deseeded
  and thickly sliced
1 green pepper, cored, deseeded
  and thickly sliced
1 onion, thickly sliced
2 tablespoons lime juice
freshly ground black pepper

NUTRITIONAL TIPS
Stir-frying is a healthy and easy way to cook. It is important to measure the oil by the teaspoon or tablespoon and use the minimum amount necessary. You can stir-fry in water, stock or wine to reduce the fat content further.

cranberry & orange turkey fillets

Preparation time: 5 minutes	Serves 4
Cooking time: 45–50 minutes	

NUTRITIONAL FACTS   ○ kcals – 330 (1386 kJ)   ○ Fat – 2 g, of which less than 1 g saturated   ○ Sodium – 120 mg

1 In a small bowl, mix together the honey, orange juice and rind, allspice and cranberries.

2 Remove all visible fat from the turkey breasts. Place in an ovenproof dish and pour half the cranberry mixture over the turkey. Bake in a preheated oven, 190°C (375°F), Gas Mark 5, for 15 minutes.

3 Remove the dish from the oven, turn the turkey pieces and pour over the remaining sauce. Return to the oven for a further 30–35 minutes. Serve with Spiced Roast Roots (see page 52) or baked potatoes and green leafy vegetables, if liked.

2 teaspoons honey
300 ml (½ pint) orange juice
1 teaspoon grated orange rind
½ teaspoon ground allspice
500 g (1 lb) cranberries (fresh, canned or frozen and thawed)
4 boneless, skinless turkey breast fillets, about 125 g (4 oz) each

NUTRITIONAL TIPS

Even when cooking lean meat such as poultry be sure to remove the fat-laden skin and trim away all the visible fat. The white meat contains less fat than the dark meat, but avoid overcooking the white meat, since it tends to dry out. Keep moist by basting with stock and wine. In many recipes chicken and turkey can easily be substituted for other lean meats, such as rabbit, venison and ostrich.

chicken enchiladas with mango salsa

Preparation time: 20 minutes

Serves 6

Cooking time: 25 minutes

NUTRITIONAL FACTS* ● kcals – 240 (1048 kJ) ● Fat – 3 g, of which less than 1 g saturated ● Sodium – 190mg

1 Heat the oil in a saucepan, add the onion and cook for about 5 minutes until softened. Stir in the beans, chicken, chillies, oregano and fresh tomato. Heat through, then remove from the heat.

2 Place the chilli powder, cumin and blended tomatoes or passata in a saucepan and simmer for 2 minutes. Remove from the heat.

3 Dip each tortilla into the tomato mixture and set aside on a plate. Fill each tortilla with 3 tablespoons of the chicken mixture. Roll up and place seam-side down in an ovenproof dish. Pour two thirds of the mango salsa over the enchiladas. Sprinkle with the cheese.

4 Bake in a preheated oven, 180°C (350°F), Gas Mark 4, for about 20 minutes. Place 2 enchiladas on each plate and serve with the remaining salsa.

2 teaspoons vegetable oil
1 large onion, chopped
250 g (8 oz) canned pinto beans, rinsed and drained
300 g (10 oz) cooked chicken breast, skinned and cubed
4 green chillies, deseeded and chopped
1 teaspoon dried oregano
1 large tomato, chopped
¼ teaspoon chilli powder
¼ teaspoon ground cumin
400 g (13 oz) can tomatoes, blended in a food processor or blender and sieved, or passata
12 corn tortillas
quantity of Mango Salsa (see page 125)
75 g (3 oz) grated low-fat mozzarella cheese

*figures per enchilada

tandoori chicken

Preparation time: 10 minutes, plus marinating   **Serves 5**

Cooking time: 20 minutes

NUTRITIONAL FACTS   ○ kcals – 212 (890 kJ) ○ Fat – 4 g, of which 1 g saturated ○ Sodium – 110 mg

1 Mix together all the ingredients for the marinade in a bowl.

2 Place the chicken in a non-metallic dish. Spoon over the marinade and rub well into the chicken. Cover and refrigerate for 2–4 hours.

3 Scrape the excess marinade from the chicken and discard. Place the chicken on a wire rack set in a roasting tray. Pour in wine or water to the depth of 2.5 cm (1 inch) and add the herb sprigs, to keep the meat moist during cooking.

4 Bake the chicken in a preheated oven, 240°C (475°F), Gas Mark 9, for 10 minutes. Turn over and bake for a further 10 minutes until cooked through. Serve with Herbed Yogurt and Cucumber Sauce (see page 140), and accompany with naan bread, basmati rice and a green salad, if liked.

4 boneless, skinless chicken
breasts, about 150 g (5 oz)
each
wine or water
a few herb sprigs, such as
rosemary, thyme or parsley

MARINADE
1 tablespoon grated fresh root
ginger
2 teaspoons coriander seeds,
toasted
2 teaspoons rosemary leaves
1 teaspoon grated lemon rind
½ teaspoon ground cardamom
½ teaspoon ground cumin
¼ teaspoon crushed black
peppercorns
¼ teaspoon chilli sauce or
powder
125 g (4 oz) natural yogurt
1 tablespoon lemon juice

NUTRITIONAL TIPS
*The tandoori marinade and
cooking method involves no
added fat or sugar and can also
be used for fish or lamb. Fish
can be cooked on a grill or
griddle for 3 minutes each side.*

turkish lamb & potato stew

Preparation time: 20 minutes   **Serves 6**
Cooking time: 2 hours

NUTRITIONAL FACTS   ❍ kcals – 307 (1290 kJ)   ❍ Fat – 10 g, of which 4 g saturated   ❍ Sodium – 384 mg

1 Heat the oil in a large, heavy-based saucepan. Add the lamb and fry, stirring, until sealed and browned all over.

2 Add the onions and garlic and fry gently for about 5 minutes until softened. Add the potatoes, tomatoes, pepper, stock or water and vinegar and bring to the boil. Add the herbs and season well with pepper. Cover and simmer gently for 1 hour.

3 Stir well, then add the aubergine and/or fennel and olives. Bring back to the boil, cover and simmer gently for 45–60 minutes until the lamb is very tender, stirring occasionally. Discard the bay leaves before serving. Serve with pitta bread and a mixed salad, if liked.

1 tablespoon vegetable oil
500 g (1 lb) lean lamb, cut into
   1.5 cm (¾ inch) cubes
4 onions, cut into wedges
2 garlic cloves, crushed
750 g (1½ lb) potatoes, cut into
   chunks
375 g (12 oz) tomatoes, skinned
   and sliced or quartered
1 red or green pepper, cored,
   deseeded and sliced
900 ml (1½ pints) stock or water
2 tablespoons wine vinegar
2 bay leaves
1 teaspoon chopped sage
1 tablespoon chopped dill or
   fennel leaves
1 aubergine and/or 1 chopped
   fennel bulb
12 pitted black olives
freshly ground black pepper

NUTRITIONAL TIPS
Beef, pork and lamb can all be part of a healthy heart diet providing the meat is extremely lean. Only eat small amounts and accompany with plenty of beans, vegetables and carbohydrates.

kofta curry

Preparation time: 25 minutes, plus chilling

Cooking time: 40 minutes

Serves 4

NUTRITIONAL FACTS   ⦿ kcals – 220 (924 kJ)   ⦿ Fat – 11 g, of which 4 g saturated   ⦿ Sodium – 96 mg

1 For the koftas, place the onion, ginger, garlic and coriander in a food processor or blender. Process until blended. Place the mince in a bowl and add the blended mixture, spices and cornflour. Knead to mix. Cover and refrigerate for 10–15 minutes, to allow the spices to infuse.

2 For the sauce, heat the oil in a heavy-based saucepan, add the onion and fry gently for 5 minutes. Add the cumin and cardamoms and cook for about 2 minutes until the onions are browned, then add the garlic and ginger paste and remaining spices. Cook, adding a little water when necessary, for about 5 minutes, until the spices darken. Add the tomatoes and yogurt, stirring continuously.

3 Meanwhile, divide the kofta mixture into 16 equal portions and roll each portion into a smooth round ball. Grill the koftas under a preheated medium grill for 10 minutes, turning once to drain off all the excess fat.

4 Add the koftas to the sauce mixture. Cook, stirring, for about 2 minutes, then add the water, cover and simmer for 20–25 minutes. Stir in the chilli and coriander, adding a little boiling water if necessary. Serve with basmati rice and Mushroom and Pea Bhaji (see page 50) if liked.

1 small onion, chopped
2 teaspoons grated fresh root ginger
3 garlic cloves, roughly chopped
3 tablespoons fresh coriander leaves
325 g (11 oz) lean lamb or beef mince
½ teaspoon chilli powder
¼ teaspoon garam masala
1 tablespoon cornflour

SAUCE
1 tablespoon vegetable oil
1 small onion, finely chopped
¼ teaspoon cumin seeds
2–3 green cardamom pods
2 teaspoons Ginger and Garlic Paste (see page 123)
½ teaspoon chilli powder
¼ teaspoon turmeric
¼ teaspoon garam masala
75 g (3 oz) tomatoes, chopped
1 tablespoon natural yogurt
450 ml (¾ pint) water
1 green chilli, deseeded and finely chopped
2 tablespoons fresh coriander leaves

bread & spread pudding

Preparation time: 30 minutes

 V

Serves 4

Cooking time: 45 minutes

NUTRITIONAL FACTS   ○ kcals – 300 (1254 kJ)   ○ Fat – 10 g, of which less than 1 g saturated   ○ Sodium – 110 mg

1 Grease a 600 ml (1 pint) pie or ovenproof dish. Cut the bread into triangles and place a layer in the bottom of the dish. Sprinkle with some of the dried fruit and a little grated orange rind. Continue with these layers, finishing with a layer of bread and spread.

2 In a small saucepan, heat the milk with the sugar until it just reaches boiling point, then allow it to cool a little. Add the orange liqueur.

3 Pour the milk mixture over the eggs in a heatproof bowl, whisking to combine. Pour the mixture over the layers of bread and let it soak for about 15 minutes.

4 Sprinkle a little sugar over the top and bake in a preheated oven, 160°C (325°F), Gas Mark 3, for 45 minutes until the top is puffed up and golden.

a little unsaturated spread, for greasing
5 slices wholemeal bread, crusts removed and thinly covered with unsaturated spread
50 g (2 oz) seedless raisins or mixed dried fruit
grated rind of ½ orange
600 ml (1 pint) skimmed milk or vanilla soya milk
25 g (1 oz) sugar, plus extra for sprinkling
splash of Cointreau or Grand Marnier
2 eggs, beaten

NUTRITIONAL TIPS
Boosting soya intake could have a major effect on reducing the incidence of heart disease. Soya milk is made from ground, whole soya beans. It is lactose- and casein-free and some brands are fortified with calcium, vitamin D and vitamin B12.

plum charlotte

Preparation time: 20 minutes   **Serves 6**

Cooking time: 40–45 minutes

N U T R I T I O N A L   F A C T S   ● kcals – 255 (1071 kJ)   ● Fat – 8 g, of which 2 g saturated   ● Sodium – 220 mg

1 Grease the base and sides of a shallow baking dish with a little of the unsaturated spread. Cover the base with some of the breadcrumbs.

2 Place a layer of plums in the dish, sprinkle with some of the sugar and a little lemon rind and juice. Dot with more spread.

3 Continue with these layers until all the ingredients are used up, finishing with a layer of breadcrumbs and dotting with spread.

4 Pour over the orange juice and bake in a preheated oven, 190°C (375°F), Gas Mark 5, for 40–45 minutes until the top is golden brown and the plums are tender.

5 Serve straight from the baking dish. Serve with low-fat custard or natural fromage frais or yogurt, if liked.

50 g (2 oz) unsaturated spread
175 g (6 oz) fresh white
  breadcrumbs
750 g (1½ lb) ripe plums, halved
  and stoned
100 g (3½ oz) soft brown sugar
finely grated rind and juice of
  ½ lemon
250 ml (8 fl oz) fresh orange
  juice

apple & fig crumble

Preparation time: 20 minutes   **V**   **Serves 6**
Cooking time: 25–30 minutes
NUTRITIONAL FACTS   ○ kcals – 250 (1050 kJ)   ○ Fat – 8 g, of which 1.5 g saturated   ○ Sodium – 75 mg

1 Sift the flour in a large bowl and lightly rub in the unsaturated spread until the mixture forms coarse crumbs. Stir in the sugar.

2 Place the fruit into a 1.2 litre (2 pint) ovenproof dish. Add the lemon rind and juice and cinnamon. Spoon the crumble mixture over the fruit and bake in a preheated oven, 180°C (350°F), Gas Mark 4, for 25–30 minutes until golden brown. Serve warm.

OR YOU COULD TRY...
Other fruit combinations. Always remember to use plenty of fruit – 500–750 g (1–1½ lb) – and sweeten slightly sour fruit by mixing with sweeter fruit, a little grated rind and juice of an orange or a variety of dried fruit. Try the following combinations:
○ Plum and blackberry
○ Rhubarb and strawberry
○ Cranberry and apple
○ Pear and blackcurrant
○ Apricot and peach

125 g (4 oz) wholemeal plain flour
50 g (2 oz) brown sugar
50 g (2 oz) unsaturated spread
500 g (1 lb) cooking apples (such as Bramleys), peeled, cored and sliced
6 dried or fresh figs, diced
grated rind and juice of 1 lemon
1 teaspoon ground cinnamon

NUTRITIONAL TIPS
Figs are high in dietary fibre, low in fat and offer a non-dairy source of calcium, iron and magnesium. They are ideal ingredients in baking, salads and make good snacks.

strawberry & fromage frais roulade

Preparation time: 30 minutes   (V)   **Serves 8**

Cooking time: 8 minutes

NUTRITIONAL FACTS   ⊙ kcals – 110 (462 kJ)   ⊙ Fat – 3 g, of which 0.7 g saturated   ⊙ Sodium – 34 mg

1 Lightly grease a 33 x 23 cm (13 x 9 inch) Swiss roll tin. Line with a single sheet of greaseproof paper to come about 1 cm (½ inch) over the sides of the tin. Lightly grease the paper.

2 In a large bowl, whisk the eggs and sugar over a saucepan of hot water until pale and thick. Sieve the flour and fold into the egg mixture with the hot water. Pour into the prepared tin and bake in a preheated oven, 220°C (425°F), Gas Mark 7, for 8 minutes until golden and set.

3 Meanwhile, place a sheet of greaseproof paper 2.5 cm (1 inch) larger than the Swiss roll tin on a clean damp tea towel. Once cooked, turn out the Swiss roll immediately face down on to the greaseproof paper. Carefully peel off the lining paper. Roll the sponge up tightly with the new greaseproof paper inside. Wrap the tea towel around the outside and place on a wire tray until cool, then unroll carefully.

4 Add half the strawberries to the fromage frais or yogurt and spread over the sponge. Roll the sponge up again and trim the ends. Dust with icing sugar and decorate with a few strawberries. Purée the remaining strawberries in a food processor or blender and serve as a sauce with the roll.

a little unsaturated spread, for greasing
3 eggs
125 g (4 oz) caster sugar
125 g (4 oz) plain flour
1 tablespoon hot water
500 g (1 lb) fresh or frozen, thawed and drained strawberries, or 425 g (14 oz) can strawberries in natural juice, drained
200 g (7 oz) natural fromage frais or yogurt
icing sugar, for dusting

NUTRITIONAL TIPS

This sponge is an absolute indulgence yet it is low in fat, the only fat being in the egg yolks. Although the cake is made with 3 eggs, each serving only contains half an egg at the most. Remember that dietary cholesterol has little effect on blood cholesterol in most people; it is saturated fat that increases blood cholesterol.

summer pudding

Preparation time: 30 minutes plus chilling   **Serves 6**

NUTRITIONAL FACTS   ○ kcals – 215 (903 kJ)   ○ Fat – 0.7 g, of which 0.2 g saturated   ○ Sodium – 270 mg

1 Cut the crusts off the bread and use to line the base and sides of a 1.2 litre (2 pint) pudding basin, fitting the pieces of bread together closely and trimming to fit. Reserve sufficient bread for the top.

2 Place the fruit, except raspberries and strawberries, in a saucepan with the sugar and water. Heat gently, until the juice begins to run from the fruit and the sugar melts. Remove from the heat, add the liqueur and remaining fruit. Drain the fruit through a nylon sieve, reserving the juice. Spoon the fruit into the lined basin with half the juices and cover with the reserved bread for the top.

3 Press the top with a weighted saucer (cover the weight with clingfilm to prevent tainting the pudding). Stand the basin in a shallow dish to catch any escaping juices and then refrigerate overnight. Cover and refrigerate the remaining juices separately.

4 To serve, remove the weight and run a blunt-edged knife around the pudding. Invert on to an edged dish, shaking gently to release the pudding. Carefully lift off the basin. Brush away areas of white bread with the reserved juices. Serve any remaining juices separately. Decorate the pudding with fruit and leaves. Serve with natural yogurt or fromage frais.

300 g (10 oz) stale medium-sliced white bread
875 g (1¾ lb) mixed ripe summer fruits, such as redcurrants, whitecurrants, blackcurrants, raspberries, strawberries and cherries, prepared separately
75 g (3 oz) caster sugar
75 ml (3 fl oz) water
a little liqueur, such as framboise, crème de cassis or kirsch
extra fruit and fruit leaves, to decorate
natural yogurt or fromage frais, to serve

NUTRITIONAL TIPS
Blackcurrants are not only very high in vitamin C but also one of the highest sources of vitamin E and therefore these small round berries are bursting with antioxidants. Every 5 blackcurrants contain 4 mg of vitamin C and 0.02 mg vitamin E.

lemon ricotta cheesecake with blueberries

Preparation time: 30 minutes   (V)   **Serves 10**
Cooking time: about 1 hour
NUTRITIONAL FACTS   O kcals – 177 (744 kJ)   O Fat – 8 g, of which 4 g saturated   O Sodium – 124 mg

1 For the crust, mix together the biscuits, sugar, cinnamon and spread in a bowl. In a separate bowl, whisk the egg white until frothy. Stir into the crumb mixture. Press into the bottom of a 23 cm (9 inch) spring form tin. Bake in a preheated oven, 190°C (375°F), Gas Mark 5, for 7–10 minutes until lightly browned. Allow to cool.

2 For the filling, place the ricotta and whole eggs in a food processor or blender and process until smooth. In a bowl, beat together the cheese mixture, sugar, yogurt, lemon juice and rind, flour and vanilla essence until well mixed.

3 In a separate bowl, beat the egg whites until soft peaks form, then fold into the cheese mixture. Spread over the crust. Bake in the oven for 50–55 minutes until the centre is firm to the touch.

4 Run a knife around the edge of the cake to loosen and allow to cool. Remove the sides of the tin, cover the cheesecake and refrigerate for at least 2 hours or up to 1 day. Just before serving, spread the top with fromage frais and cover with blueberries or other fruit.

500 g (1 lb) skimmed ricotta
  cheese
2 large eggs
75 g (3 oz) sugar
150 g (5 oz) natural yogurt
4 tablespoons lemon juice
grated rind of 2 lemons
2 tablespoons plain flour
2 teaspoons vanilla essence
2 egg whites
150 g (5 oz) natural fromage frais
300 g (10 oz) fresh, frozen and
  thawed or canned, drained
  blueberries or other soft fruit

CRUST
125 g (4 oz) plain digestive-type
  biscuits, crushed
2 tablespoons sugar
1 teaspoon ground cinnamon
15 g (½ oz) unsaturated spread
1 egg white

mango & pineapple pavlova

Preparation time: 20 minutes   (V)   **Serves 4**
Cooking time: 1 hour
NUTRITIONAL FACTS   ○ kcals –245 (1029 kJ)   ○ Fat – less than 1 g, of which negligible saturated   ○ Sodium – 77 mg

1 Whisk the egg whites in a bowl until they are stiff. Fold in
1 tablespoon of the sugar, then gradually whisk in the remainder.
The meringue must be glossy and form peaks when spoonfuls are
dropped into the bowl. Fold in the black coffee.

2 Spread the meringue mixture over a large sheet of baking paper
to form a 20 cm (8 inch) diameter round. Make a slight hollow in the
centre of the meringue and cook in a preheated oven, 120°C (250°F),
Gas Mark ½, for 1 hour until the meringue is crisp. Remove from the
oven and leave to cool on the paper for about 10 minutes before
peeling off.

3 When the meringue is cold, fill the hollow in the top with
fromage frais. Arrange the mango and pineapple on top, then drizzle
the passion fruit seeds and juice over the fruit.

OR YOU COULD TRY...
These other combinations of fruit to fill the pavlova:
- Strawberries and mango
- Raspberries and blueberries
- Cherries and nectarines
- Pineapple and papaya

3 egg whites
175 g (6 oz) caster sugar
1 teaspoon strong black coffee
250 g (8 oz) natural fromage
     frais
125 g (4 oz) mango, diced
125 g (4 oz) fresh pineapple, cut
     into chunks
1–2 passion fruits

NUTRITIONAL TIPS
*Pavlova, a much-loved dessert,
is surprisingly very low in fat.
Meringue is naturally a very
low-fat choice since it is made
from egg white. You can replace
a whole egg with two egg
whites in most recipes or use
dried egg white powder. Use
fromage frais instead of high
fat cream and add any variety
of fruit that you like. Orange
and yellow fruits, such as
mangoes and pineapples, are
bursting with ACE antioxidant
vitamins.*

prune & chocolate crunch

Preparation time: 15 minutes

 V

Serves 12

Cooking time: 30 minutes

NUTRITIONAL FACTS   ○ kcals – 165 (693 kJ)   ○ Fat – 2 g, of which less than 1 g saturated   ○ Sodium – 75 mg

1 Blend the prunes and water in a food processor or blender until almost smooth. Alternatively, mash with a fork.

2 Grease a Swiss-roll type baking tin. Place the prune purée and the remaining ingredients, except those for the topping, in a large bowl and mix well.

3 Spread the mixture evenly in the tin and bake in a preheated oven, 180°C (350°F), Gas Mark 4, for about 30 minutes. Leave to cool in the tin.

4 Before the crunch is completely cold, mix together the ingredients for the topping in a bowl, then spread over the crunch. Cut into 12 squares.

125 g (4 oz) stoned prunes
4 tablespoons water
a little unsaturated spread, for greasing
150 g (5 oz) self-raising flour
125 g (4 oz) porridge oats
75 g (3 oz) sugar
3 teaspoons cocoa powder

TOPPING
100 g (3½ oz) icing sugar
2 teaspoons cocoa powder
a little orange juice

NUTRITIONAL TIPS
Cocoa is another source of antioxidant polyphenols, similar to those found in fruit, vegetables, red wine and tea, and may have heart-health benefits. Unfortunately, it is also very high in fat and sugar. Puréed prunes are a perfect fat substitute to use in baking. Just substitute the purée for butter or margarine on a direct weight-for-weight measure. Prunes also provide fibre, iron, potassium and vitamin A.

pure fruit cake

Preparation time: 15 minutes
Cooking time: 1½ hours

  Makes 12 slices

NUTRITIONAL FACTS   ○ kcals – 218 (916 kJ)   ○ Fat – 2 g, of which less than 1 g saturated   ○ Sodium – 145 mg

1 Grease a 1 kg (2 lb) loaf tin. Place the dates in a saucepan with the measured water and heat gently until they are soft. Remove from the heat and mash with a fork until puréed.

2 Place the date purée in a bowl with all the remaining ingredients, except the flaked almonds, and 4 tablespoons of water. Mix together well. Spoon the mixture into the prepared tin and level the top. Sprinkle with flaked almonds.

3 Bake in a preheated oven, 160°C (325°F), Gas Mark 3, for 1½ hours until a skewer inserted into the middle comes out clean. Towards the end of cooking you may need to protect the top of the cake with foil.

4 Allow the cake to cool a little in the tin, then turn out and finish cooling on a wire rack.

a little unsaturated spread, for
  greasing
250 g (8 oz) stoned dates
300 ml (½ pint) water
175 g (6 oz) seedless raisins
125 g (4 oz) sultanas
125 g (4 oz) currants
50 g (2 oz) candied mixed peel,
  chopped
175 g (6 oz) wholemeal plain
  flour
3 teaspoons baking powder
1 teaspoon mixed spice
grated rind and juice of 1 orange
  or lemon
25 g (1 oz) ground almonds
a few flaked almonds, to
  decorate

banana & raisin tea bread

Preparation time: 10 minutes   (V)   **Serves 12**

Cooking time: 50 minute–1 hour

NUTRITIONAL FACTS   ● kcals – 190 (798 kJ)   ● Fat – 7 g, of which 2 g saturated   ● Sodium – 110 mg

1 Grease a 1 kg (2 lb) loaf tin. Melt the spread in small saucepan over a low heat. Sift the flours, baking powder and cinnamon into a large bowl. Stir in the sugar, mashed bananas, melted spread, raisins and eggs and beat for 3 minutes until smooth.

2 Turn the mixture into the prepared tin and bake in a preheated oven, 180°C (350°F), Gas Mark 4, for 50 minutes–1 hour until a skewer pierced through the centre comes out clean. Stand the tin on a wire rack to cool slightly before turning out.

3 The tea bread is much tastier if left to mellow for 2–3 days wrapped closely in foil. It can be served thinly sliced and spread with low-fat soft cheese or made into sandwiches with thinly sliced apple or mashed banana.

75 g (3 oz) melted unsaturated spread, plus a little extra for greasing

150 g (5 oz) wholemeal self-raising flour

75 g (3 oz) wholemeal plain flour

1 teaspoon baking powder

1 teaspoon ground cinnamon

75 g (3 oz) brown sugar

3 bananas, well mashed

100 g (3½ oz) seedless raisins

2 eggs, lightly beaten

NUTRITIONAL TIPS

Research shows that a dietary pattern with more servings of fruit, vegetables, grains, nuts and beans, with an emphasis on foods that provide potassium, calcium and magnesium, helps prevent high blood pressure. All fruit and vegetables are good sources of potassium, but particularly bananas, dried fruit, apricots, rhubarb, blackcurrants, pulses, baked beans, beetroot, sweetcorn, mushrooms, spinach and potatoes.

basic recipes

vegetable stock

Preparation time: 20 minutes
Cooking time: 1 hour 45 minutes
Makes 2.7 litres (4¾ pints)

3 medium onions, roughly chopped
5 medium carrots, roughly chopped
3 medium leeks, coarsely sliced
3 medium celery sticks, roughly chopped
3 cabbage leaves, sliced
1 head of lettuce, sliced
6 sprigs of flat leaf parsley with stems, roughly
   chopped
3 sprigs of thyme
1 bay leaf
3.6 litres (6 pints) cold water

1 Place all the ingredients in a saucepan or
stockpot. Cover and bring slowly to the boil.
Reduce the heat to a gentle simmer. Skim off
any scum. Simmer very gently, covered, for
1 hour, skimming from time to time. Do not
disturb or move the stock in any way.

2 Strain well, being careful not to force any of
the ingredients through the sieve, since this will
cloud the stock. Allow to cool, then cover and
refrigerate.

O fat-free

O Sodium – 90 mg

chicken stock

Preparation time: 10 minutes
Cooking time: 2–3 hours, plus chilling
Makes 2.5 litres (4 pints)

1.5 kg (3 lb) fresh chicken
1 onion, stuck with three cloves
2 carrots, coarsely sliced
2 celery sticks, coarsely sliced
1 head of garlic, cloves separated and unpeeled
6 sprigs of flat leaf parsley with stems
3 sprigs of fresh thyme
1 bay leaf
2.75 litres (5 pints) cold water, to cover chicken
   by at least 7 cm (3 inches)

1 Place all the ingredients in a large saucepan
or stockpot. Cover and bring slowly to the boil.
Reduce the heat to a gentle simmer. Skim off
any scum. Simmer very gently, partially covered,
for 2–3 hours for a rich stock, skimming from
time to time. Do not disturb or move the stock
in any way.

2 Strain well, being careful not to force any of
the ingredients through the sieve, as this will
cloud the stock. Allow to cool, then cover and
refrigerate for several hours before removing all
the solidified fat.

O fat-free

O Sodium – 94 mg

olive vinaigrette

Preparation time: 5 minutes
Makes 300 ml ('/. pint)

125 ml (4 fl oz) balsamic vinegar
125 ml (4 fl oz) lime juice
2 garlic cloves, crushed
3 black olives, pitted
1 tablespoon Dijon mustard
pinch of sugar

1 Place all the ingredients in a screw-top jar, replace the lid and shake well. Store in the refrigerator for up to 7 days.

○ kcals – 82 (344 kJ)
○ Fat – 3 g, of which less than 1 g saturated
○ Sodium – 800 mg

fruity dressing

Preparation time: a few minutes
Makes 100 ml (3'/. oz)

2 teaspoons wholegrain mustard
4 tablespoons balsamic vinegar
1 tablespoon olive oil
1 tablespoon orange or apple juice
freshly ground black pepper

1 Place the wholegrain mustard, balsamic vinegar, olive oil, orange or apple juice and pepper in a screw-top jar, replace the lid and shake well to combine. Store in the refrigerator for up to 7 days.

○ kcals – 130 (340 kJ)
○ Fat – 12g, of which less than 2 g saturated
○ Sodium – 166 mg

ginger & garlic paste

Preparation time: 5 minutes
Makes 250 g (8 oz)

125 g (4 oz) fresh root ginger, peeled and cut
    into chunks
125 g (4 oz) peeled garlic cloves

1 Process the ginger with the garlic cloves in a food processor or blender with a very little water, to aid processing. Spoon into an airtight screw-top jar and store in the refrigerator for up to 3 weeks. Alternatively, place small quantities in a specially reserved ice-cube tray, or spread the paste on to a baking sheet, freeze, then remove the slab and break into pieces. Store in a plastic freezer bag.

○ kcals – 184 (773 kJ)
○ Fat – 2 g, of which less than 1 g saturated
○ Sodium – 19 mg

teriyaki sauce

Preparation time: a few minutes
Cooking time: a few minutes
Makes 100 ml (3½ oz)

1 shallot, finely sliced
1 teaspoon minced fresh root ginger
50 ml (2 fl oz) rice wine vinegar or sherry
2 tablespoons reduced-salt soy sauce
1 teaspoon honey
2 tablespoons lime or lemon juice
1 teaspoon sesame oil

1 Place the shallot, ginger, vinegar or sherry, soy sauce, honey and 1 tablespoon lime or lemon juice in a small saucepan over medium heat. Stir in the sesame oil and remaining lime juice and heat through.

O kcals – 140 (588 kJ)
O Fat – 3 g, of which less than 1 g saturated
O Sodium – 10 mg

herbed yogurt & cucumber sauce

Preparation time: 5 minutes, plus chilling
Makes 2–3 servings

125 g (4 oz) grated cucumber
1 tablespoon chopped dill or mint
200 g (7 oz) natural yogurt
1 tablespoon lime or lemon juice
freshly ground black pepper

1 Mix the ingredients together, cover and chill in the refrigerator for about 30 minutes before serving to allow the flavours to develop.

O kcals – 125 (525 kJ)
O Fat – 2g, of which less than 1 g saturated
O Sodium – 170 mg

tomato salsa

Preparation time: 10 minutes, plus infusing
Makes 8 servings

500 g (1 lb) ripe tomatoes, skinned and
　deseeded
1 small onion, finely chopped
1–3 green chillies, deseeded and finely chopped
1 tablespoon white vinegar
pinch of sugar
2 tablespoons chopped fresh coriander or
　parsley
freshly ground black pepper

1 Finely chop the tomatoes by hand or process
very briefly in a food processor or blender. Mix
with the remaining ingredients. Leave for
30 minutes for the flavours to infuse. The salsa
will keep for up to 7 days in the refrigerator.

○ kcals – 115 (483 kJ)
○ Fat – 2 g, of which less than 1 g saturated
○ Sodium – 50 mg

mango salsa

Preparation time:10 minutes, plus infusing
Makes 6 servings

1 mango
200 g (7 oz) ripe tomatoes, skinned, deseeded
　and chopped
1 green chilli, deseeded and finely chopped
1 tablespoon chopped mint
1 tablespoon chopped fresh coriander leaves
juice of 1 lime
1 tablespoon olive oil
pinch of sugar
freshly ground black pepper

1 For the salsa, cut the mango lengthways
either side of the thin central stone. Cut away
the skin from the flesh. Finely chop the flesh
and place in a bowl with the tomatoes.

2 Add the remaining salsa ingredients. Cover
and refrigerate for at least 30 minutes to allow
the flavours to infuse. (The salsa will keep for up
to 7 days in the refrigerator.)

○ kcals – 266 (1114 kJ)
○ Fat – 13.4g of fat of which 1.8g is saturated fat
○ Sodium – trace

index

acknowledgements

Thank you to all at the Family Heart Association, especially Michael Livingston for giving me time to write this book and Gill Stokes who gave me some of her family's favourite recipes. To all at The Conquest Hospital, Hastings, my friends and colleagues in The Nutrition and Dietetic Department for their departmental recipes and to Alison Hassell, Senior Dietitian for working with me on 'Making Changes'. To all in Cardiology, especially Dr Richard Wray, Cardiologist for his constant support and encouragement, the Cardiac Rehabilitation Team and all my patients over the years whom I have been privileged to meet and who have taught me so much. To my own dear children, Lottie, Sam and Tom, for their resilience – it can't be easy having such a 'passionate' dietitian for a Mum! Finally, to Jonathan for his love, hours of patience and help with this book.

THE AUTHOR

Jacqui Lynas (BSc SRD) is a state-registered dietician with a specialist interest in heart-disease prevention. She works for the Family Heart Association and is an acknowledged expert in her field with over 20 years' experience. She is a regular contributor to medical textbooks, journals and magazines, as well as being a popular speaker at scientific meetings.

Photographic Acknowledgements in Source Order

Getty Images 5 top right, 5 bottom, 9 top, 9 bottom, 15 bottom Octopus Publishing Group Limited/David Jordan 17 detail 1/William Lingwood 16 detail 1, detail 2/William Reavell 1, 5 top left, 10 bottom, 12 top, 12 bottom, 13 top, 14 top, 14 bottom, 15 top, 16 detail 3, 16 detail 4, 16 detail 5, 16 detail 6, 17 detail 2, 17 detail 3, 17 detail 4, 17 detail 6, 17 detail 7, 20 top centre, 20 top right, 21, 23, 27, 28 top centre, 28 top right, 31, 35, 39, 40 top centre, 40 top right, 43, 47, 51, 54 top centre, 54 top right, 55, 59, 63, 66, 70 centre, 70 top right, 71, 75, 77, 81, 83, 86 top centre, 86 top right, 87, 91 95, 99, 100 top centre, 100 top right, 103, 107, 108 top centre, 108 top right, 111, 115, 117, 121/Simon Smith 17 detail 5. Science Photo Library 7 top, 7 bottom.

For Hamlyn

Executive Editor **Nicky Hill**
Editor **Alice Tyler**
Senior Designer **Peter Burt**
Designer **Mark Stevens**
Special Photography **William Reavell**
Home Economist **Louise Blair**
Picture Researcher **Zoë Holterman**
Production Controller **Aileen O'Reilly**